# RUNNING
## WITH
# WOLVES

### OUR STORY OF
### LIFE WITH THE
### SAWTOOTH
### PACK

## JIM & JAMIE **DUTCHER**
### WITH GLEN PHELAN

WASHINGTON, D.C.

Text and photographs Copyright © 2019 Jim and Jamie Dutcher

Compilation Copyright © 2019 National Geographic Partners, LLC

Since 1888, the National Geographic Society has funded more than 12,000 research, exploration, and preservation projects around the world. The Society receives funds from National Geographic Partners, LLC, funded in part by your purchase. A portion of the proceeds from this book supports this vital work. To learn more, visit natgeo.com/info.

For more information, visit nationalgeographic.com, call 1-800-647-5463, or write to the following address:

National Geographic Partners
1145 17th Street N.W.
Washington, D.C. 20036-4688 U.S.A.

Visit us online at nationalgeographic.com/books

For librarians and teachers: ngchildrensbooks.org

More for kids from National Geographic: natgeokids.com

*National Geographic Kids* magazine inspires children to explore their world with fun yet educational articles on animals, science, nature, and more. Using fresh storytelling and amazing photography, *Nat Geo Kids* shows kids ages 6 to 14 the fascinating truth about the world—and why they should care. kids.nationalgeographic.com/subscribe

For information about special discounts for bulk purchases, please contact National Geographic Books Special Sales: specialsales@natgeo.com

For rights or permissions inquiries, please contact National Geographic Books Subsidiary Rights: bookrights@natgeo.com

Designed by Sanjida Rashid

Map, pp. 4-5: Evelyn B. Phillips; Map, pp. 154-155: National Geographic Maps; Illustration, pp. 156-157: Fernando G. Baptista.

The publisher would like to thank everyone who made this book possible: Kate Hale, executive editor; Paige Towler, associate editor; Mike McNey, cartographer; Shannon Hibberd, senior photo editor; Sally Abbey, managing editor; Joan Gossett, editorial production manager; and Anne LeongSon and Gus Tello, production assistants.

Hardcover ISBN: 978-1-4263-3358-3
Reinforced library binding ISBN: 978-1-4263-3359-0

Printed in U.S.A.
18/QGF-QGL/1

# NOTE

Jim and Jamie Dutcher grew up in different places, but they both loved exploring the great outdoors. They had a passion for observing wildlife that continues to this day. Along with that passion comes immense respect for wild animals, and for their wildness. If you see a wild animal, be respectful just like Jim and Jamie. Observe the animal from a safe distance and don't disturb it. Let it be wild.

In this memoir, Jim and Jamie each tell different parts of their adventures with wolves. Jim tells much of the first half because Jamie didn't join the wolf project until its third year. Yet, she was always very much a part of it. Long before she arrived at wolf camp, Jamie helped keep the project on a steady course through advice and encouragement offered in letters and phone conversations. Many of these communications are recalled in this story.

For our grandchildren, Arianna,
Sofia, Natalie, Sebastian, and Emiko;
our nephew, Sam-Henry; and our
niece, Madeline. And for young people
everywhere—may you always follow
your dreams. Together, we can make
a difference for the natural world.

*—Jim and Jamie Dutcher*

trapper's cabin

lodgepole
pines

fir
trees

meadow
where wolves
play

willows where
lakota hid

chemukh's
den

makuyi's
hiding place

aspen groves

N

where cougar
jumped fence

EBPhillips

# TABLE OF
# CONTENTS

# A WOLF'S TRUST

## JAMIE

I stood silent and motionless, my eyes trained on the mysterious black hole in front of me. The opening was just two feet (0.6 m) wide, half hidden beneath a fallen spruce tree. Its oval shape reminded me of a dark, mystical eye, like that of a dragon. Such a thought of fantasy contrasted sharply with the reality of what I was about to do. It was something that no one had likely ever done.

I sniffled against the chilly April air. Spring had sprung a month earlier, according to the calendar anyway. Somewhere nourishing rains and lengthening days were coaxing flowers to show their colorful faces. Somewhere tree buds were awakening from their long winter rest, and grass was once again growing green.

Somewhere, but not here. Snow still covered most of the ground in the forest that surrounded me. The warmth of the season comes late, and slowly, to the mountains of Idaho.

I glanced at my husband, Jim, through a cloud of my condensed breath. He crouched nearby behind his movie camera. All of his years as a filmmaker led up to this moment, and he wasn't about to let it slip by without capturing it on film.

Looking up from his eyepiece, he nodded. I walked cautiously toward the gaping black hole. With each step, I became more aware of the sounds around me. The gentle rush of a breeze and the chirping of black-capped chickadees mingled with the crunching and squishing of snow and mud under my boots. My own heartbeat reverberated through several layers of clothing.

There were other sounds, too. Distinct chirps, almost birdlike, pierced the frigid air. The source was unseen, distant yet nearby, but I knew what it was. So did the wolves.

Seven big and powerful gray wolves were gathered around the opening, pacing back and forth and trampling the ground into a muddy mess. They couldn't go in—they instinctively knew that—so they took turns peering into the hole as they whined with excitement.

As I slowly reached the wolves, they made way for me, as if I were one of them. I knelt down on the damp ground and stared at the opening. Barely a minute went by. Then suddenly a wolf poked her head out. Her yellow eyes set against her black face were like two piercing lights. The sight would have startled—and maybe frightened—most people. But I knew those eyes well. They looked curious … intelligent … calm.

The black wolf emerged completely, revealing her full size. She greeted me with a tender whine, gave me a little lick on the nose, and sat beside me. We looked at each other. I gently spoke and asked if I could go where she had been. I tried to read her body language for any signs of fear or uncertainty. Was she annoyed that I was here? Would she attack me? She never had, but today was unlike any other, and quite frankly I wanted to make sure she wouldn't bite me on the behind.

Her expression seemed only to say, "It's okay, go on in. I trust you."

That was the invitation I was hoping for. I took out a small flashlight from my jacket pocket and showed it to her. She inspected it and seemed satisfied that it posed no threat. I smiled and took a deep breath. Then I flicked on the light, lowered my head, and leaned in …

Why was I about to squeeze myself into this dark, damp hole in the ground? What did I expect to find? Stranger still, why was a large, powerful wolf sitting calmly beside me as I prepared to enter a place so precious to her that even other wolves were not allowed?

The answers to these questions are at the heart of this story. It's a story of our adventures. It's a story of our struggle and survival and the wolves' struggle and survival, but also of trust, friendship, and even love. It's a story of what happens when two people decide it would be a good idea to spend six years living in the wilderness with a pack of wolves. 🐾

## CHAPTER 1

# LONGING FOR WILDERNESS

## JIM

I tugged gently on the worn leather reins, and Glendora, my buckskin mare, came to a slow halt. She turned her head to look back at me and I leaned down in the saddle to give her a reassuring pat on the neck. We both knew we had a job to do, but the view was just too spectacular to miss. I needed a minute to take it all in.

It was first light—my favorite time of day. The sun had just peeked above the horizon and its glorious rays began to illuminate the landscape. A beautiful lake shimmered in the growing light. Its smooth surface mirrored perfectly the fast-changing colors of the early morning sky—from golden yellow to deep pink to rich azure blue. Bright wildflowers dotted the green grassy meadows that surrounded the lake.

What dominated the landscape, though, were the mountains. In almost every direction, forests swept up to the base of sheer rocky cliffs that reached at least 2,000 feet (610 m) toward the sky. Most of the mountains formed walls of layered rock, like those of the Grand Canyon, rather than peaks. The ashen gray cliffs looked dull compared to the rich palette of the valley below.

But sunlight is nature's artist, and it can turn a colorless canvas into a dazzling masterpiece. That's what I was waiting to see on this clear, chilly summer morning. As the sun inched its way into the sky, the light crept down the east-facing cliffs to my right, transforming the somber gray first into a rosy pink and then a brilliant orange. The rock seemed to glow. The effect soon passed, but as always, it was breathtaking.

I looked south across the lake to the ranch on the far shore. Then, taking a deep gulp of fresh mountain air, I sat up straight in the saddle, thought for the umpteenth time how lucky I was, and announced to my trusty companion, "Okay, Glennie, let's round up these ponies."

The year was 1959. I was 16 years old and had the summer job of a lifetime—I got to be a cowboy! Well, a wrangler actually. A cowboy herds cattle; a wrangler herds horses.

I worked on a ranch in the high country of Wyoming. By "high country," I mean the ranch sat at 9,200 feet (2,804 m) above sea level. There, among the peaks of the Absaroka Range, I felt like I was on top of the world. The location couldn't have been more perfect. The ranch sat on a hill above the mountain lake. Beyond the ranch stood a deep green forest of pine. The views were awe-inspiring no matter where I was, and not only at first light.

Then, as now, this part of the Rocky Mountains was far less known than the nearby tourist attractions of Yellowstone National Park. That was just fine with me. I could roam and explore the pristine wilderness without seeing a single person. That is, once my daily chores were done.

Each evening before sundown, I would drive a herd of about two dozen horses from the ranch to a meadow on the other side of the lake. There I would leave them to graze, drink from a cool mountain stream, and sleep peacefully among the willows and meadow grasses.

Then every morning I had to go get the horses and take them back to the corral. This wasn't a job for anyone who liked to sleep in. I would rise from my bunk bed well before dawn and dress quickly— not only because I wanted to hit the trail but also to stay warm. At this high elevation, the early morning air was cold, and usually I wore two pairs of jeans, a long-sleeve shirt, and a jacket. My leather gloves and cowboy hat also provided some warmth.

I really didn't mind the cold weather, though. In fact, for a kid who grew up in subtropical Florida, these cool summers were welcome, even exhilarating.

So, looking every bit the part of a movie cowboy, I'd ride Glendora back to the meadow just as the faintest glimmer of light began to tinge the dark eastern sky and the jagged peaks of the Pinnacle Buttes. The well-rested horses would usually be on their feet by the time we arrived, finishing a breakfast of soft, dew-covered grass.

I'd circle around to the far side of the herd and push them together in the direction of the ranch. I didn't literally *push* the horses. Instead, I'd come up from behind and call out "Hee-yah!" Off they'd gallop. I would feel the rumble through my body as their hooves pounded the ground.

Sometimes the horses would spook and bolt in another direction. Glendora would take off after them with little coaxing from me. It's a good thing she knew her job so well, because during these hard gallops I could do little more than hang on for dear life.

Eventually we'd round up the herd. Then I'd ride behind or alongside the horses to guide them the two miles (3 km) back to the corral for the day.

That was the general idea, anyway. When you're dealing with animals, things don't always go according to plan.

Often, I'd discover that other large animals, hidden from view, had visited the herd during the night—and they were sticking around for breakfast.

You might not think a meadow could provide much cover for anything larger than a ground squirrel or a mouse. But the willows were a bit taller than me and grew in tangled bunches, like dense bushes. Even sitting high in the saddle, it was difficult to see more than just the backs of the horses grazing in between the willows. It wasn't until I started flushing the horses out that I noticed some of them didn't look like the others. Some had antlers! To my surprise, I realized that I was rounding up not only horses but also a few very confused moose.

I felt sorry for them. The moose must've been completely bewildered, wondering why their breakfast had been disturbed by a stampede—and why they were in the middle of it! Sorry or not, I had to separate these wild animals from the herd.

Easier said than done.

Moose aren't usually aggressive, but if they feel harassed or threatened, watch out! They can kick their sharp, pointed hooves forward, backward, and sideways. I didn't want to be on the receiving end of one of those powerful thrusts. And I sure didn't want to mess with those antlers. They were wider than my arm span. One quick move of the moose's neck and his massive bony headgear could crush my leg or Glendora's skull. I didn't dare get too close.

So instead of separating the moose from the herd, I separated the herd from the moose, pushing the horses away as I normally did. Now and then, the moose followed or ran with the herd for a while. Maybe they didn't want to leave their new companions. Or maybe they just wanted to see where everyone was going. Whatever the reason, their stomachs usually won out, and they'd trot back to the meadow for breakfast.

Dealing with moose tested my horse-riding skills and helped keep the job from ever becoming boring. Not that there was much chance of that happening. Something was always keeping me on my toes.

If moose weren't visiting the meadow, strays were leaving it.

Strays were horses that wandered off early in the morning, before I got to the herd. I knew each of the 28 steeds in my charge and could tell quickly when one or more were missing. It always seemed to be the same restless few that wandered, so I had tied bells around their necks earlier in the summer for easy tracking.

One day, several horses had wandered off into the forested hills on the other side of the meadow. After driving the rest of the herd back to the ranch, I returned to collect the strays.

It was so quiet. Away from the herd, the ranch, and anything with a motor, I could hear the slightest sounds—the shriek of a hawk high above or the trickling of a winding brook. So it was no surprise that I picked up the faint tinkling of bells coming from the forest across the meadow. Glendora and I followed the distant *ding, ding, ding* up into the foothills.

These were my favorite times. Tracking strays gave me a chance to explore the countryside. The cool air, the wilderness, and the freedom were all so new to me, and thrilling. I was living my dream of roaming the Great American West.

That morning we searched more than usual as we followed the bells farther and farther into the Wyoming backcountry. It was slow going. We blazed our own trails as we picked our way through forests, creeks, and clearings. Wooded ravines were the toughest to navigate. I leaned back in the saddle to make the downslope easier on Glendora. Then she quickly scooted up the other side. On hard ground, I stopped every few minutes so that the *clip-clop* of horseshoes didn't drown out the distant sound of bells.

We were an hour or so into our journey. The sun had climbed higher in the sky and I welcomed the growing warmth. I pushed aside a low-hanging branch as we stepped out of the forest into a large clearing. Suddenly we stopped in our tracks.

Beyond the clearing, groves of dark green lodgepole pines gave way to a steep grassy slope strewn with boulders from the rock formation that towered high above: Brooks Mountain. Its majestic cliffs rise 1,300 feet (396 m) straight up. This mass of rock stretches for more than a mile and is part of the Continental Divide—the long line of high elevations that zigzags its way north and south across the continent and separates river systems that flow to the Pacific from those that flow to the Atlantic.

I had seen Brooks Mountain many times, and it always struck me as magnificent, but at that moment, something else caught my attention.

Across the clearing stood a coyote.

It's not that the sight of a coyote was a heart-stopping shock. It wasn't. All sorts of animals big and small roamed the countryside. I had seen eagles soaring above the cliffs, black bears nibbling berries, herds of elk grazing in open meadows, and more.

Coyotes were common, too, but they were skittish. Ranchers hunted them, afraid that the carnivores would harm their livestock. Consequently, coyotes had learned to quickly run away when they saw or smelled a human approaching.

Not this coyote. He and I were having a staring contest.

He didn't seem the least bit afraid, just curious about this two-legged creature sitting atop a four-legged creature across the meadow.

Something else was different about him. Even from a distance I could tell that he was larger than any coyote I had ever seen. His legs were longer and his face broader.

Then it hit me. This wasn't a coyote at all. It was a wolf!

Glendora became restless. She snorted and neighed, shook her head several times, and stepped in place nervously. "Easy, girl," I said as I gently patted her neck. Glendora calmed down, but I wanted a closer look, so I coaxed her to slowly follow the edge of the clearing and head toward the wolf.

I learned two things about wolves that day—they're smart and they're curious. While we circled the edge of the clearing, the wolf did, too, in the same direction so as to keep the same distance between us. His yellow eyes stayed locked on mine as we both circled the meadow. Eventually we each ended up where the other had stood.

The wolf inspected where Glendora had trampled the grass. He showed no signs of fear, no signs of aggression, only cool curiosity. What were we? Were we a threat? He seemed to be pondering these questions. I watched, fascinated, and wondered what conclusions he had drawn.

I couldn't take my eyes off this large, furry, doglike creature—a predator that I had long heard was an aggressive, vicious, unforgiving killer. I saw none of that. All I saw was intelligence and fearlessness ... but only for a minute longer. Then, the wolf simply turned and trotted away and disappeared among the pines.

Eventually, I found the stray horses. They were safe and sound, but I never saw the wolf again. No wonder. I later discovered that seeing a wolf at that time in that place—my very first wolf sighting—had been an incredibly rare event. In 1959 as few as 15 wolves lived in the U.S. Rocky Mountains, and I had seen one of them. I wouldn't see another for 30 years.

And when I did, it would change my life forever.

# JAMIE

The zookeeper burst through the doorway. The front of her T-shirt was untucked, with the bottom folded up like a soft taco shell, and her hands clearly cradled an object within.

"It's a joey!" the keeper exclaimed. An involuntary gasp escaped my lips as the keeper revealed the precious cargo she was carrying—a tiny, hairless baby kangaroo.

"What happened?" my colleagues and I asked in unison.

"The mother rejected him," she replied hurriedly. "I don't know why."

The keeper, sweating on this hot day in May at Smithsonian's National Zoo in Washington, D.C., quickly explained that the mother kangaroo had kicked the joey out of her pouch. A visitor had seen the horrifying incident and contacted the zookeeper, who rushed into the enclosure, picked up the squirming youngster, and brought him to me and two other keepers at the zoo hospital.

The baby kangaroo was no bigger than the length of my hand. Like all joeys, he would normally live inside his mother's pouch for six months after birth before developing enough to venture outside now and then. But this poor little guy, who we called Rufus, was only three months old and completely helpless. He would never survive without the care of his mother—or without the care of three determined zookeepers.

We were the only chance Rufus had. We had to mimic the conditions of a mother kangaroo in every possible way, including the soft, moist, and warm environment within her pouch. But how?

Part of the answer was clear—make a substitute pouch. We fashioned a number of comfortable pouches out of soft cotton pillowcases.

To hold in body moisture, we covered Rufus with a special kind of skin cream. For warmth, we placed him inside one of the cotton pouches and set it in a heated incubator about the size of a large aquarium.

Food presented another set of challenges. Baby kangaroos eat every two hours, day and night, and Rufus was no exception. We mixed up a nutritious formula that was similar to his mother's milk. Then we fed him using baby bottles topped with nipples that were the length and shape of his mother's.

Joeys have a weak immune system, so we took every precaution to prevent infections. Each time we fed him or handled him for any reason in those first few months, we wore surgical gowns, gloves, and masks. We washed and bleached his pouches after every feeding so there would always be a stack of them ready to use.

To provide the round-the-clock care that a joey needs, we took turns taking Rufus and his incubator home every evening. Those were sleepless nights. After donning my surgical garb, feeding Rufus, wrapping him in a fresh pouch, getting him settled, and changing my clothes, I'd barely close my eyes before it was time to do it all over again.

Needless to say, after such a night I was groggy the next morning at work. So what better way to shake off the cobwebs than to hop around the office? Literally. A few times each day, I or one of the other "kangaroo moms" would cradle Rufus in his pouch and hop around our hospital office for a few minutes. Not just any old hop, either. No, this was a regular dance. *Hop, hop, hop,* dip to the left. *Hop, hop, hop,* dip to the right. Repeat and repeat and repeat!

The dance was hilarious. It was also absolutely necessary. The hopping mimicked the movements Rufus would have received inside his mother's pouch. Such movements are essential to develop the joey's circulatory and digestive systems. And that's what we explained to any perplexed visitor who happened by the office in the middle of a kangaroo dance.

All of the loving care paid off. Rufus grew into a healthy and playful young kangaroo. After six months or so, we no longer had to cradle him. Instead we hung his pouch on a doorknob, and he could hop in and out as he pleased.

I can still see him grabbing the pouch, launching himself off the floor, and diving in headfirst. A hodgepodge of limbs and tail stick out for a brief moment, then disappear inside. The pouch churns like a tongue rolling against the inside of a cheek. Suddenly up pops a head. The mischievous look on his face was priceless.

So was the experience of caring for this little life. Rufus took us on an exhausting, emotional roller coaster, and I wouldn't have traded the wild ride for anything. Taking care of Rufus and other at-risk creatures at the zoo was never a job to me—it was a passion, a passion born out of my love for animals.

That love began long before I ever dreamed of working at the zoo. In fact, it was evident to others when I was only a few years old, when my hands held not animals but crayons.

The first recognizable picture I ever drew was an elephant. At least, that's what my grandmother told me, and I believe her. When I wasn't drawing pictures of animals, I was reading about them. If there was an animal on the cover, that's the book I opened. Even well into my teens, I would trade a mystery or adventure novel for a book about animals any day.

Drawings and stories sparked my imagination, but what I enjoyed most were my outdoor adventures, where I was in the animals' world. As a young girl, I loved exploring the woods behind my house in suburban Washington, D.C., searching for wildlife. Those woods were my wilderness. I could lose all track of time wandering among the oak and hickory trees, turning over fallen leaves and peeking under logs in search of salamanders and frogs.

I kept my eyes peeled for snakes, too. Not to avoid them, but to get a good look at them! They didn't give me the willies like they do some people. Instead, I was mesmerized by their colors and patterns, by how they moved and what they did.

My suburban wilderness was also home to larger animals, like white-tailed deer. But that's not all. When I was seven years old, I heard that someone had spotted a black bear in a nearby wooded park. I searched those woods for days. I imagined what I would say to the bear if we met. No doubt we would like each other. In fact, I let myself believe that we would become friends.

I never did find the bear. And as I grew older and learned more about wildlife, I realized that a human and a wild animal could not become friends. At least, that's what all the experts said.

My passion for wildlife only grew. After college, I tried to settle down and live a "normal" life, apart from all things wild. But animals were never far from my mind. I longed to be part of their world. So, in my mid-20s, I made two decisions that allowed me to follow my passion.

First, after working at a small-animal clinic, I decided to apply for a job at the National Zoo. There at the hospital I took care of sick, injured, or other at-risk animals, like Rufus.

The second decision ended up being the most monumental one of my life. I took a trip to Africa.

I traveled with a friend to Zimbabwe to photograph some of that African country's amazing wildlife. I had always enjoyed photography, and this was a chance of a lifetime to see elephants, gazelles, lions, and other wild animals in their natural setting. The trip was phenomenal, but the most significant moments took place on the way home.

My friend and I were boarding a plane in London to begin the second leg of the long journey back to Washington. With my backpack flung over my shoulder, I was trying to avoid banging into other passengers as I shuffled my way down the aisle. I was about to pass a man placing a bag in the overhead compartment. Suddenly he looked at me and asked, "Have you been in Africa?"

I had a deep tan and was wearing a beaded necklace of coral and warthog tusk. Clearly, I couldn't have gotten the tan or the necklace in London, so with a smile and a good-natured touch of sarcasm, I responded, "Yes, what gave it away?"

He smiled back and mentioned my necklace. Then he started asking about my trip. Where had I been? What animals had I seen?

But a narrow plane aisle with annoyed passengers piling up behind us was no time or place for an extended conversation. So, after a few brief answers, I continued to my seat a dozen rows back.

Every day people have brief encounters that they never think about again. It might be chitchat in the checkout line at the grocery store or a pleasant exchange of "Thank you" and "You're welcome" while holding open a door for a stranger. This easily could have been one of those forgotten encounters.

Fortunately, the man who had struck up a conversation with me wanted to continue it. After we reached cruising altitude, he looked back, unclasped his seat belt, and walked down to my aisle seat. He greeted me with a sweet smile and a kind "Hi again."

We talked easily. He too was on his way back from Africa. He had been visiting his sister in Kenya, where she and her husband operated a tented camp in a remote area. We swapped stories of the African animals we had seen. Through our tales, we relived the wonder of the wildlife and the respect for the natural order of things that we had witnessed on the African savanna.

I immediately launched into a story about when I saw a pack of five spotted hyenas splashing through marshy waters to steal a zebra carcass from three lions. It was like an old-fashioned sword fight.

The hyenas attacked first. Then the lions withdrew, dragging most of the kill with them. Ever the opportunists, the hyenas snatched up a few hunks of meat left behind, then withdrew a few feet themselves.

Not satisfied with their meager scraps, the hyenas made another charge. Their high-pitched hums and whines sent a shiver down my spine. Instantly one of the lions surged forward with a ferocious roar and scattered the thieves. But they immediately regrouped, chased away the lions, and claimed their prize—the rest of the carcass. Victors: hyenas!

My new friend listened with rapt attention. Then, with his blue eyes sparkling, he described in vivid detail how a cheetah had chased down a gazelle. As he spoke, I could smell the dust kicked up from the dry grasses and feel the relentless heat of the sun. I saw the rippling muscles of the cheetah as she hunted the nimble gazelle. With his hands, my friend pantomimed how the cheetah gobbled up ground with bursts of speed as fast as a car on the highway.

I immediately knew I was in the presence of a gifted storyteller.

Not surprisingly, he revealed he was a filmmaker. In fact, at that moment he was finishing a film about the life of beavers for National Geographic. He told me he was on his way to their headquarters in Washington to discuss the film's progress.

The more we talked, the more we enjoyed each other's company. Our common interests certainly helped. In addition to being a filmmaker, he was, like me, a photographer, a bird-watcher, and passionate about wildlife. I was also taken by his smile, his laughter, and his kindness.

Then we got separated.

In the mad rush of people getting off the plane in Washington, I lost sight of this man whom I wanted to know more about. I didn't even know his name. With a sigh I resigned myself to the fact that we would never see each other again. Our relationship would be no more than pleasant conversation to pass the time on a long plane ride.

Fate appeared to have other ideas.

As I joined a hundred other people at baggage claim to get my luggage, I turned—and there he was! We both beamed in recognition, and relief, and picked up our conversation. He told me more about his wildlife films, and I told him that I had applied to work at the National Zoo.

And we finally introduced ourselves. Now I had a name to put with the face of Jim Dutcher.

Despite the bond we felt for each other, we lived in two different parts of the country, almost in two different worlds. After Jim's business in Washington, he was heading home to Idaho.

*Idaho!* I never would have guessed it. I had nothing against this western state, of course. It's just that I didn't know anything about it, except that potatoes came from there. My mind flashed back to grade school and the maps that showed the main products from each state. I pictured the map of Idaho with potato icons scattered about.

For an Easterner like me, who had never been west of the Mississippi River, Idaho seemed as remote as Africa. I couldn't imagine life there.

Little did I know that in a few years' time, Idaho would be the place where all my dreams would come true. 🐾

## CHAPTER 2

# A BRIGHT IDEA

## JIM

Long before the thought of living with wolves ever entered my mind, and even before I met Jamie, I honed my skills as a wildlife filmmaker. My first films were undersea adventures. I focused on the colorful fish that live among the reefs off the shores of my native Florida.

As beautiful and fascinating as I found the ocean, I was drawn to the forested mountains of the West. My teenage experiences as a wrangler fed my desire to film some of the animals that live there—like beavers.

These creatures are usually either underwater or in their lodges, making them tough to spot in the wild. So instead, for my movie, I built a beaver lodge inside a log cabin. I was able to film—from the other side of a large window—the comings and goings of a beaver family and show the world these quirky animals' daily activities. I even filmed the birth of beaver kits.

The subject of my next film was a larger and decisively more dangerous animal. It was also much more elusive, almost to the point of being ghostly.

The cougar grasped the neck of the deer in her powerful jaws as she dragged the limp body through the dry pine needles and sparse clumps of grass. When she released her grip, the lifeless animal hit the ground with a thud.

The deer had been struck and killed by a vehicle—a certain tragedy for the deer and most likely a harrowing experience for the driver. For the cougar, it was a week's worth of meals. But the food wasn't only for her.

Three male cougar kittens watched with interest from the shadows of a nearby rocky perch. Their spotted youthful coats made them difficult for the naked eye to see. But my telephoto lens clearly caught their expressions, which seemed to say: "Here's something new."

Until this point, the six-week-old kittens' nutrition had come exclusively from their mother's milk. It was now time to wean them away from nursing. As carnivores, they needed to experience the taste of meat. This would be their first.

The mother looked up toward her kittens and sounded the call for dinner. *Meow! Meow!* Remarkably similar to the mewing of a household cat, the call of the cougar was nonetheless sharper, shorter, and more determined. To my ears it sounded like she was saying "Now! Now!" and was not about to take no for an answer.

The kittens dutifully heeded the call. Placing one furry oversized paw in front of the other, they gingerly stepped down from their perch toward this new lesson in survival.

Meanwhile, the mother prepared the meal the way mother cougars do. She cleaned a portion of the deer's belly by removing the fur and tough skin with her raspy tongue and teeth to expose the fresh meat for her kittens. Then she took a few bites and walked away.

This was the part of the lesson the kittens had to learn for themselves—how to actually eat prey.

They approached the deer steadily but cautiously. One batted it with his paw, perhaps testing if it was really dead. Another tugged at one of the deer's large pointy ears. He kept gnawing on the tough leathery appetizer, ignoring for the moment the entrée his mother had prepared on the other side.

The kittens not only had to get used to solid food but also had to learn how to chew and swallow it without eating the fur. Now and then, a kitten gagged, opening his mouth wide and releasing a harsh *Ack!* from his little throat.

I couldn't help but smile behind the camera. It was thrilling to capture this brief snippet of cougar life. It was one of many rare glimpses into the hidden world of this magnificent animal. I was documenting behavior that few if any humans had ever witnessed. Every moment was new and surprising ... and priceless.

How was I able to get such intimate footage of an animal that was seldom seen in the wild, let alone filmed? Not by chasing after it, that's for sure.

I had better methods in mind. And the lessons I learned from making my cougar film would prove to be invaluable, especially when I began studying wolves several years later.

The idea to focus on cougars came from Jamie. I was in Washington for meetings while finishing the beaver film. As usual, Jamie and I met for lunch while I was in town. I wanted my next project to be about a big cat—perhaps cheetahs in Africa.

Jamie suggested cougars instead. These animals go by many names—mountain lion, puma, catamount. The idea intrigued me.

I had never seen one in the wild, but I knew they were out there, roaming the same forests and mountainsides that I called home. I later discovered that Jamie had steered me toward cougars partly to keep me in the country. I was glad she did.

While planning the cougar project, I knew that I would have to bring the cougar to me. That meant filming in an enclosure—a large fenced-off area on the edge of wilderness. I didn't want to fool anyone. I would make it clear in the documentary that I was using an enclosure, and in fact, make the enclosure part of the story. I'd let the viewer "in on the secret" by revealing how I was making the film.

I envisioned creating a semiwild situation in which a mother cougar and her kittens would be accustomed to my presence and allow me to film them without changing their behavior. While the cougars could not pursue large prey or roam without boundaries, they would be free to hunt small animals, communicate, show affection, and interact as a family.

With such a secretive animal, these behaviors would have been impossible to film in the wild. But in a large enclosure, I could film and record up close the sights and sounds that no one had ever seen or heard. Such an intimate look at this illusive animal would make people value it and want to protect it. That was my goal.

It was a tall order.

First on the to-do list was finding a site to build the enclosure. Working with a biologist, we found the perfect place—five acres (2 ha) of government land in the White Cloud Mountains of central Idaho.

The U.S. Forest Service granted my crew the land for a two-year study. The site was suitably rugged and included huge boulders, groves of aspen and pine trees, open grassy land, a stream, and a pond. We set wooden posts in the ground and connected them with chain-link fencing. Three tents just outside the fence would be our home for two years.

We also had a plan for the cougar's food—roadkill. We arranged for local authorities to notify us when a large animal had been struck on the road by a vehicle. Then we'd head out, scoop up the carcass, and bring it to the enclosure for the cougar to find and feast on.

It was a good setup and a good plan. Now all we needed was a cougar.

After a long search, we located a 110-pound (50-kg) female. She had been raised in captivity, yet she maintained her wild nature. Perhaps she was a bit too wild or simply too much to handle, because the owner was going to have her put to sleep!

Upon hearing such disturbing news, the zoo in Boise, Idaho, bought the cougar. But the zoo had little space for her, and officials there were delighted to let us provide her with a home.

Two things made this cougar the ideal choice: One, because she had been raised in the presence of humans, she was already used to having people around. Two, she was pregnant. The kittens would be born in just a few months.

I could hardly wait. How does a mother cougar interact with her kittens every day? How does she care for them? What does she teach them? I had so many questions, and I wanted to capture the answers on film and show the world.

The pickup truck backed up to the entrance of the enclosure. It was a warm day in late spring. I let out a grunt as I helped ease the steel crate off the truck and gently onto the ground. I slid open the door of the crate and the feline mother-to-be walked out calmly without even looking at us.

Good. The less attention paid to us the better.

The bright sunshine made the cougar's tan fur glow golden. Her impressive muscles flexed with each stride as she went about exploring her new home. Using her sharp claws and long tail for balance, she skillfully crossed streams on fallen tree trunks. Her powerful magnificence made me gasp. Then she trotted away into the aspens and disappeared. Compared to the pen in which she had been raised, this habitat offered boundless freedom.

We gave her a few hours to acclimate to the new surroundings, and then set off on foot to find her.

It wasn't easy. With the cougar's keen sense of smell and sharp eyesight, I'm sure she knew where we were practically at all times. By comparison, our senses were dull, and we had to look and listen with all the intensity we could muster. She knew how to hide just by being still. No doubt she was lying low, uncertain that we meant no harm.

Finally, we spotted her. She crouched in the tall grass barely 20 yards (18 m) away—a distance that she could close in two leaps if she wanted to.

We made eye contact. The big cat remained absolutely frozen, watching our every move intently. Suddenly I felt vulnerable, more so than I ever had. I knelt down slowly with my camera hoisted on my shoulder. My sound technician Peter, with his equipment, and my assistant Jake, carrying a large stick, did the same.

The cat continued to eyeball us from her crouched position. Then she raised and wiggled her hindquarters. That got me nervous. Anyone who has seen similar behavior from a house cat getting ready to pounce could guess what happened next ...

She suddenly sprang.

We quickly rose to our feet, terrified. This wasn't a squirrel or a fox coming our way; it was one of nature's strongest, fastest predators, and she had us in her sights. We started yelling as loud as we could, "Hey! Hey!" and "He-yah! He-yah!"

I exhaled with relief as the cougar suddenly veered off in another direction. But, my relief was short-lived.

She stopped, turned around, and looked at us again. Was she going to make another run at us? My heart was pounding. My knees became almost too wobbly to hold the camera steady. But we stood our ground. Then without warning, she attacked.

With long strides, the cougar ran right at Jake and wrapped her muscular forelimbs around his waist. The force of the impact knocked the stick from his hands. He twirled reflexively to break away, but the cat held on, hopping on her hind legs to maintain balance as she also twirled. It was like a dance, but one that could have deadly consequences.

The cougar looked like she was going to climb up on Jake's back when Peter ran to Jake with his microphone boom raised like a baseball bat. The threatening stance seemed to do the trick, because the cougar released her grip and ran off.

Jake was shaken but unharmed, a sign that the cougar did not intend to hurt him. She most likely was just playing a cat-and-mouse game, following her urge to stalk and test her skills. That sort of game can turn out badly for the mouse, so I was deeply concerned for the safety of my crew.

Not that it kept us away. Each day, we entered the enclosure to look for the cat, to observe and film. She never attacked us again. Maybe she just wanted to send a message during that first encounter. Message received!

We kept our distance and she kept hers, at first. But each day we inched closer and closer. Soon she got used to our presence and we reached a level of comfort and trust.

In fact, as time went on, the cougar even displayed affection. She would sometimes press her body against my leg and purr. It wasn't a quiet purr like a household cat makes; her purr was more like an idling motorcycle.

At other times, she would stalk and chase us in a friendly game of cat and mouse. Well, friendly to her—we were the mice. We had gotten used to these games and were no longer fearful. But, we were always on our guard and watchful of any sudden change in behavior.

Our trusting relationship developed just in time, for soon the cougar gave birth to three male kittens.

We found the den amid a sheltered rocky outcrop. The kittens were just minutes old. Their spotted fur blended in with the ground, offering some protection against other predators. The helpless kittens' eyes were closed and their little ears lay flat against their head. The newborns would remain blind and completely dependent on their mother for 10 days.

One by one, she gently picked them up by the scruff of their neck in her jaws and laid them in a soft bed of pine needles. Then she cleaned them with her large, rough tongue. When a kitten cried out with a squeaky *rahr, rahr*, the mother gave a few more reassuring licks.

These were the intimate sights and sounds I most wanted to capture, like the mother nursing her kittens—a tender moment perhaps never seen with cougars in the wild. There were many such moments of peace and tranquility between parent and young. There were other moments of high-energy training between teacher and student.

For instance, one day I watched with keen interest as a kitten tugged at one of his mother's ears while she lay on the ground. Playing along, she gently laid a massive paw on his head like she was petting him. Then he saw her tail—a long rope of fur waving lazily in the air. It was like the tail was daring the kitten to grab it. The kitten took his chance and pounced. He bit and pawed at the tail for a few seconds, until his mother decided enough was enough and brushed him aside.

Every moment of play was actually a valuable lesson. The growing kittens were learning how to stalk and take down prey by sneaking up on each other and play fighting. These bouts were like friendly wrestling matches, but with teeth.

By autumn, the kittens were learning to hunt real prey, from mice in the fields to ducks on the pond. They were becoming increasingly wild, too.

They hid from me more often, and hissed when I approached. I was glad. One day they would be released into the wilderness, and I didn't want them to get too comfortable with people. I didn't want them to get used to having a harmless camera pointed at them, either. Hunting cougars is legal in many western states, and the next piece of equipment that was pointed at them might be a rifle.

When I started the cougar project, there was no guarantee of success. A lot could've gone wrong. The mother might never have accepted me, or the crew, into her world. She may have chosen to hide her young from the watchful eye of my camera lens. Or she may have turned aggressive, making the project too dangerous to continue.

Fortunately, none of these things happened. We were able to show the cougar not only as a powerful hunter but also as a nurturing parent and a patient teacher. We even revealed the sounds of the cougars' world—from the chirps, purrs, mews, and growls of their language to the shoulder-shivering scrapes of the sharpening of the mother's claws against a tree trunk.

The following spring, the young cougars reached the age when they normally go their separate ways. They were ready.

The mother was too familiar with humans to survive in the wilderness, so she was taken to a large preserve to live out her days in safety. The young cougars had a less predictable but more natural future.

We flew them by helicopter to a remote area of Idaho. Thanks to instinct and lessons learned as kittens, they were now self-sufficient and able to live a truly wild life. They stepped from their crates and never looked back. In a few days, the brothers would head in different directions to establish their own territories. They were free.

My cougar adventure was over, but theirs were just beginning.

*What next?* That's what I asked myself as we removed the fencing and any trace of human activity at the cougar enclosure.

I was itching to start another project. As before, I wanted to do something that would inspire people to care about wildlife. The best way I knew how to do that was to make another film about the hidden daily life of an animal. It would have to be an animal that was largely misunderstood, an animal that was rarely filmed in the wild.

But, which animal?

To help me decide, I thought a little vacation was in order. Not Disney World or a Caribbean cruise. No, I needed a sense of peace— the kind of peace I get from a place of quiet natural beauty, a place where I could clear my mind. I decided to return to the Wyoming ranch in the Absarokas.

More than 30 years after I had spent the summer as a wrangler, I returned as a guest. For company, I had a stack of books about animals. I was going to pore over them for a few weeks in between hiking and fishing. Somewhere in the research and the inspiration of the mountains, I figured I'd find the subject of my next film.

I didn't know the answer would hit me like a lightning bolt.

On the second day of the trip, I received a phone message that my cougar film, called *Cougar: Ghost of the Rockies,* had been chosen as the first episode of a nature TV series. I was overjoyed. I felt like a 16-year-old again, full of boundless energy.

I had the irresistible urge to make a climb that had been one of my favorites as a teen. I remembered that the view at the top was spectacular. I stepped my way through a stand of white pines to the base of a hill. I scrambled up the rocky slope, hunched over to keep my balance. At the top, I stood up straight to take in the view. Suddenly, I froze like a statue.

On the alpine meadow below me stood a gray wolf.

In a flash, my mind raced back to that day 30 years earlier when I had seen my first wolf. Now, in the same area, I was looking at my second. Could this be a descendant? I wondered about the possibility as I raised my binoculars to get a closer look. That's when he saw me. Unlike the wolf that stared me down years before, this one was skittish and ran away at the sight of me.

In that brief moment, I knew that I had found the subject of my next film. I still didn't know much about wolves, but I was about to begin a journey that would make me an expert in ways I never thought possible.

The first step in that journey was to separate fact from fiction. And when it comes to wolves, I learned that there was very little fact and a whole bunch of fiction.

Like most people, much of what I knew—or thought I knew—about wolves was based on the sayings, songs, movies, and fairy tales I had learned since childhood. A "wolf in sheep's clothing" is someone whose pleasant personality hides sinister motives. In the fairy tale "Little Red Riding Hood," a wolf devours a grandmother and tries to trick her granddaughter into a similar fate.

Horror movies about werewolves—bloodthirsty half-man, half-wolf creatures—have been popular for generations. And who is trying to blow down the houses of the Three Little Pigs and eat the occupants? The Big Bad Wolf, of course!

Such stories and sayings show the wolf as a tricky, ferocious, evil creature—one to be feared, hated, and destroyed. Among those who held such perceptions were ranchers, as well as farmers who raised livestock. If a cow or sheep went missing, wolves were usually blamed.

Not that it *never* happened. These predators sometimes did kill a member of a herd, but the culprit was much more likely to be disease, weather, injury, or a predator other then a wolf, including domestic dogs.

I wasn't completely surprised to learn how make-believe stories fed people's misconceptions about wolves. But I was astounded and alarmed to learn how false perceptions had affected the wolf population. From the mid-1800s to the mid-1900s, about two million wolves had been killed in the United States, largely because they were seen as a threat to livestock. In fact, in 1915, the U.S. government hired hunters and called for the extermination of wolves.

It almost happened.

The government paid hunters for each wolf they killed. By the time I started to research my wolf film, this beautiful animal that once inhabited forests and plains from Maine to California existed only in small pockets of the United States. At the most, no more than a handful of wolves roamed the entire American West. Even though they were protected under the Endangered Species Act of 1973, their numbers were still dangerously low.

More importantly, attitudes about wolves had changed little, especially among the ranchers and big-game hunters who shared the environment with this animal. It was personally disheartening. These were my neighbors and friends, yet our views of wolves were very different. Many people still considered them to be aggressive killers. But the more research I uncovered, the more I saw wolves as curious, intelligent, and even shy. I knew they were getting a bad rap.

I couldn't really blame people for their attitudes, though. Myths die hard, especially in the absence of truth.

In 1990, we knew surprisingly little about the nature of wolves. We had measurable facts—things that you could attach a number to—like a wolf's size, how far it roams, how long it lives, things like that.

We knew wolves live in packs, but we had little idea about *how* they live. We knew almost nothing about the secret, hidden lives of wolves. I needed to change that. I needed to show people a side of wolves they never saw, never even knew existed. Perhaps that information would help replace myth with truth.

I felt the only way to discover that truth was to live with wolves.

So, I decided to assemble a wolf pack to observe and film within the world's largest wolf enclosure. I had no idea what I was getting into and how difficult the road ahead would be, but I knew that I was doing the right thing. I was certain that if only someone would take the time to listen, the wolf would tell its story. I was willing to listen.

So was a certain zookeeper in Washington, D.C.

Jamie and I had kept in touch ever since we met on a trip home from Africa three years earlier. She was as excited as I was when I told her about my plans to live with wolves. We both knew this was a much more ambitious undertaking than the cougar project, and she understood why I had to do it.

In the early days of the project—before Jamie joined me in Idaho—I depended on her advice and support through letters and conversations. I still remember the joy I felt as I wrote her with some thrilling news. 🐾

## CHAPTER 3

# BEGINNINGS
## OF THE
# SAWTOOTH PACK

## JIM

*"I found it!"*

That was my message in a nutshell.

In a letter to Jamie, I described how I had found the perfect place to build wolf camp. It was in the Sawtooth Mountains, across the valley from where cougar camp had been.

I had explored other mountain ranges in central Idaho, but I could never find a place that had everything the wolves would need. Then I discovered Meadow Creek. It's an area of meadows, forests, creeks, marshes, and ponds, all near the base of the Sawtooth Mountains.

This place was really off the beaten path. I took a dirt road across two ranches, and when the road ended, I got out and walked. The landscape changed dramatically as I hiked up a slight incline. It's amazing the difference a little change in elevation makes!

Instead of the dry sage of the ranches, I suddenly found myself in a green, grassy meadow.

It was like a piece of paradise. A mountain brook trickled past me on my left while bright yellow aspen leaves twisted and turned in the breeze on my right. In front of me stood a deep green forest of towering lodgepole pine, Douglas fir, and spruce. And above that rose the majestic Sawtooths. Their summits formed a jagged gray ridge against the deep blue sky.

Meadow Creek had everything I could want. It was remote enough that people wouldn't wander by and disturb the wolves. In fact, people would have a hard time finding this place even if they were looking for it. Yet the site could be reached by an equipment truck, which would be needed to haul in materials to build the enclosure.

The whole area was also extremely picturesque, with a variety of landscapes. That was important to me as a filmmaker.

The fiery oranges and golds of autumn were brilliant. The colorful spring flowers and summer shades of green would be no less spectacular. And the hushed winter beauty of a snow-covered forest would perfectly reflect the wolf's connection to wilderness. This site had everything my camera would love.

Most importantly, it had everything wolves would need. Sunny meadows offered places to run and play. The forest provided hiding places where they would feel safe. Ponds and streams supplied water for drinking. Rocks and fallen trees presented a choice of den locations, in case one of the wolves gave birth to pups someday.

No doubt about it—Meadow Creek was the perfect setting for wolves. But there was more to consider.

The site was reachable only by driving across private land. I worried that the two ranchers whose land we would have to cross wouldn't exactly be thrilled with having a pack of wolves nearby.

But I was pleasantly surprised. They were interested in the project, and they granted my crew and me permission to come and go across their land. I was glad to see that not all ranchers were at war with wolves.

Some were. Before the project started, we were warned that people who didn't want wolves around could make trouble for us. Someone might even go as far as to shoot the wolves through the fence or throw poisoned meat into the enclosure. Because of those frightening possibilities, we took every precaution to keep the location secret.

One hurdle remained—getting permits. Meadow Creek was public land; I didn't own it, and I couldn't just fence off part of it and start the project.

I received a permit from the U.S. Forest Service easily enough, but I also needed one from the Idaho Department of Fish and Game. I wasn't looking forward to facing the Fish and Game commissioners. They and I well remembered what happened after my cougar film.

In *Cougar: Ghost of the Rockies,* I included a scene that showed hunters tracking down a cougar and killing it. Many hunters were outraged with that part of the film, claiming that it made them look unfairly cruel; some even left me threatening phone messages.

The Fish and Game commissioners got an earful from hunting groups who were angry with the department for giving me a permit to conduct the cougar project in the first place. Meanwhile, environmental groups criticized Fish and Game for allowing the hunting of cougars. My film had put the commissioners in the middle of a cougar controversy, and they didn't want a repeat performance with wolves.

So I wasn't optimistic as I sat down in front of the five commissioners to explain my wolf project and answer their questions.

"What happens if a wolf escapes?" one wanted to know. "Who will be held responsible if it kills a deer?" asked another.

In the end, they issued me a permit. To the commissioners' credit, even though they knew the film might cause them problems, they also knew it would've been wrong to censor a filmmaker. I was grateful, and relieved.

Now I could move forward.

I had marked off 25 acres (10 ha) even before I had the permits. The wolf enclosure would be the world's largest and encompass meadows, aspen groves, pine forests, willows, streams, and ponds.

Construction began in the spring. As we unloaded the huge piles of posts and rolls and rolls of chain-link fencing from the flatbed truck, it struck me just how big 25 acres is and how enormous this project was going to be.

Fortunately, I had the help of a hardworking crew and my good friend Jake. He was the carpenter who had designed the beaver lodge and cougar camp for my previous projects. Jake could build just about anything. Good thing, too, because I really needed his skills when it came to the fence.

After we dug the holes, set the posts, and nailed the chain-link, I looked at the fence and thought, *This isn't going to work.* I kept picturing a wolf going over it, under it, or through it.

My first concern was the height of the fence. I had settled on 10 feet (3 m). That looked ridiculously high in summer. But in winter, snow could pile up to my shoulders. Then a 10-foot fence wouldn't look so secure. It still would be difficult for a wolf to scurry up and over the remaining fence height, but not impossible.

I worried even more about a wolf going *under* the fence. Wolves are terrific diggers. They could be under and out of a typical fence in half an hour.

So I had to make sure the fence wasn't typical.

To discourage the wolves from digging, we attached a section of chain-link near the bottom of the fence that curved several feet into the enclosure. Any wolf that tried to dig its way out would have to excavate a tunnel under this chain-link apron before reaching the main fence. That would be too much even for a determined wolf.

Finally, I imagined a wolf prying open fencing where two sections met. So we attached clamps—32,000 of them—along these seams. Problem solved.

As it turned out, I had worried for nothing. Not a single member of the Sawtooth Pack ever tried to get out or even paced the perimeter. True, their spacious territory was an ideal place to live, but the place was not the reason for their contentment. The reason was the pack itself. I'd come to learn that each wolf knew that it belonged with the pack, with the family.

Next, we turned our attention to the rest of the camp and what the crew would need to survive in the wilderness. Camping for a week or two on summer vacation is one thing. Camping for years at a time, through all seasons, is quite another. Every crew member chipped in with ideas for how to make the camp functional and comfortable.

I based the overall layout of the camp on a safari camp my sister had in Africa. That meant separate tents for sleeping and cooking.

Unlike conditions in Africa, however, winter weather in the Sawtooths can be brutal, and we needed tents that were up to the challenge. Janet, my associate producer, suggested we use a yurt.

"A what?" I asked.

No one else had heard of it, either. Janet, who was an expert in cold-weather survival, explained that a yurt is a round tent about 16 feet (5 m) wide with a cone-shaped roof. They are used by nomads in the central Asian country of Mongolia. The conical roof along with a sturdy wooden frame allows the yurt to withstand blasts of wind and the weight of heavy snowfalls.

Our yurt worked perfectly as the winter kitchen, work area, and year-round storage tent. In the summer, we used a larger cook tent but dismantled it as winter approached and moved the kitchen items to the stronger yurt.

We built three other tents for sleeping. These were more traditional in design, but like the yurt, they had sturdy wooden frames for support.

Nights were chilly in summer and bitterly cold in winter. Yet the tents were comfy and cozy—as long as the firewood kept burning.

Our heat came from burning wood in a small woodstove in each tent. Dead trees provided plenty of firewood, but it was up to us to saw it and split it into pieces that fit in the stove. In winter, that was probably our most important chore. Well, in addition to shoveling a path to the smallest tent in camp—the outhouse. When nature calls in the middle of a winter night, no one wants to stumble through snow to answer it.

Personal touches made camp life more enjoyable. Jake's wife, Patty, furnished the camp with a wild assortment of items she had purchased at garage sales. Thanks to her, tables had colorful tablecloths, and candles sat in all kinds of fun candlesticks. The old railroad lanterns she brought lit many an evening as the crew gathered around the table to share thoughts, stories, and laughs.

Patty also became the main chef, though everyone pitched in at mealtime and took turns preparing food. Salmon, pizza, and chicken dishes were among the mouthwatering favorites.

Wolf camp had no electricity, plumbing, or gas lines, and yet we had everything we needed. A small tank of propane gas provided the flames to cook our food. Oil lanterns gave us light to read by, and candlelight produced a softer glow for conversation.

Drinking water was brought in with our supplies by snowmobile or all-terrain vehicle. Water for washing came from the stream or melted snow. We even built a shower tent. It included solar-heated bags of water hung above a wooden grate. When you live and work closely with people, staying clean makes life more pleasant for everyone.

Through ingenuity and creativity, we made life at wolf camp fairly comfortable. In fact, some visitors thought it was too cushy, that we weren't roughing it enough.

I could practically read their minds. *How dare you sleep on comfortable foam pads in homemade beds? You should be in sleeping bags on the hard ground outside. How can you call it camping when you cook delicious meals of chicken and pasta? Shouldn't you be surviving on dried fruits and nuts? You know, like* real *campers!*

I had to smile when someone brought it up. Usually it was a young intern who was helping out for a few weeks as part of a college course. I explained that our intent was not to live *like* wolves; it was to live *with* wolves, and in a way that disturbed them and the environment as little as possible. Only then might the wolves open their lives to us.

By creating a camp that was well organized and comfortable, my crew and I were free to do our work, whether that was cleaning precision equipment, brainstorming a sequence for the film ... or making arrangements to adopt the very first members of the Sawtooth Pack.

I shielded my eyes from the sun as I scanned the distant skies. The mountains were as beautiful as ever, but on this day, I was looking for something else ...

Then I heard it—the drone of a distant engine.

A few seconds later, sunlight glinted off the wings of the small two-seater and I pointed: "There it is!" I knew the plane actually sat four, but the rear seats had been removed to make room for a very special passenger.

The plane landed on the runway, which was nothing more than a dusty strip of worn grass in a field. When the engine stopped, I rushed over and barely greeted the human occupants before looking at the adult male wolf in the back of the plane.

"Is he okay?" I asked with concern.

He was fine, though heavily sedated and lying on his side in a metal cage.

We carefully transferred the cage to Jake's pickup and drove to wolf camp. The biologist who delivered the wolf carried him across his shoulders, with the tail hanging down one side and the head down the other. We entered the enclosure and gently laid him on the grass in a clearing among a stand of aspens.

That's when it struck me: For the first time in more than 50 years, a wolf was back in the Sawtooth Mountains.

His name was Akai (ah-KYE), which means "wise one" in the language of the Native American Blackfoot tribe. Akai was the first, but he wouldn't be the last.

Even while we were constructing camp, plans had been under way to assemble the wolf pack. Janet located Akai at a wolf education center in Ely, Minnesota. At about the same time, we found Makuyi (mah-KEW-ee).

Makuyi (Blackfoot for "wolf") took me by surprise. I first saw her in a Montana wolf shelter. Her owner, Karin, had rescued a group of wolves from a research lab several years earlier. Makuyi was the offspring of two of them. I was completely captivated by her beauty, her grace, and her sweet personality. I had never been affected this way by the other animals I had observed, not even a magnificent cougar and her cuddly kittens. But this wolf, I simply adored. It was my first hint that I was doing something very special and beginning a lifelong adventure.

A few weeks later, I walked through the gate of the enclosure cradling Makuyi in my arms. Like Akai, she was sedated, and she lay in the grass until the drug wore off.

Akai had been placed in a "lock-off" section of the enclosure. There he stayed for an hour or so until Makuyi awoke and got accustomed to her new home. Then I released Akai.

I didn't know how they would respond to each other. Would they get along, or would they fight?

Akai hadn't been in the enclosure long, so I didn't think he would defend the land as his territory. Besides, in the wild, if an adult male were alone, he likely would be searching for the companionship of other wolves. He especially would welcome the company of a female wolf, like the sweet Makuyi. Still, I wasn't sure.

My concerns quickly subsided. The two wolves approached each other warily but not aggressively. Instead, they greeted each other with a few tender licks of the nose and mouth, called the muzzle.

The pack was off to a good start, but something was missing—pups.

It just so happened that, along with five-year-old Makuyi, Karin from the wolf shelter had four of the most adorable wolf pups that anyone could ever hope to see. They were 10 days old. Their eyes had barely opened.

These little balls of fur became the first pups of the Sawtooth Pack.

*Hi Jamie,*

*It's early morning at wolf camp. A wolf was howling as I built a fire in the tent stove only minutes ago. The weather is clear and cold. The temperature got down to the mid-30s last night even though it's late June. As always, the mountains behind camp look spectacular.*

*I'm writing this letter from within the wolves' territory. I'm trying to bond with Akai and Makuyi, so I'm spending as much time as possible just being with them. Here I sit leaning against an aspen tree, with a gorgeous mountain as a backdrop and two wolves tilting their heads trying to figure out what I'm doing.*

*Akai and Makuyi seem to be getting along well enough. Makuyi appears to be quite fond of her pack mate. She'll often follow him around the meadow or over by the ponds. She usually greets him in the morning with a lick of the muzzle or a slight nudge of the shoulders. Akai barely returns the affection. Sometimes I think he's just tolerating her.*

*But I know you want to hear about the pups. Here's the latest.*

*I am overjoyed with them! I'm also a bit overwhelmed. What an incredible responsibility! Now I know how you felt when you took care of Rufus. The pups keep us going 24 hours a day. Fortunately, between my crew and I there's no shortage of people to take care of them.*

*Just like you did with Rufus, we have to imitate everything a mother would do. We clean the pups with warm, damp rags to mimic a mother wolf's tongue and we supply them with plenty of blankets so it feels like their mom's warm, cozy fur.*

*Because the pups will need our constant care, they will live with us at both wolf camp and at my home in Ketchum. Whenever we need to resupply camp, they will come with us to reinforce our bonds and keep them safe.*

*By the way, thank you so much for the milk formula recipe. The pups love it. They gobble it up, or I should say, slurp it down. After bottle-feeding, they fall fast asleep in our laps.*

*I have to go. It's my turn to nurse the pups.*

*Cheers,*

*Jim*

*P.S. Wow, I just learned a lesson. Never leave anything unattended around wolves, like this letter. Akai tried to steal it. See the tooth puncture mark in the center of the page. Lucky I got it back!*

My knowledge of raising wolves grew out of a friendship I had with a fellow filmmaker in Germany. He had raised a captive pack and stressed that trust was the most important ingredient in forming a safe and healthy pack—trust that could only be achieved by living with the wolves as a social partner.

This was a new idea for me, and a challenging one. I had hoped that, as with the cougars, I could simply let these wolves live their lives without human interference. But cougars and wolves are very different creatures. These wolves must trust me absolutely or my work would be impossible. I was going to have to be more involved in their lives than I had anticipated.

With this trust in mind, I had decided to hand-raise the pups for the first several weeks. From what I was learning, the pups had to get used to my crew and me from the moment they opened their eyes if the project was going to succeed. That meant we had to live with the pups for a while before we could let them live with Akai and Makuyi.

I don't think any of us were prepared for the physical demands of raising four wolf pups. It seemed the only times they were calm were when they were sleeping. When awake, they were little whirlwinds of fur tearing around our tent. Their high-energy antics kept us on our toes ... and smiling every minute.

Anything they could get their paws on or sink their teeth into became a toy. I learned quickly that an open container, no matter how high off the floor, was an invitation to mischief.

A sample sequence of events in our cook tent went something like this:

- 🐾 Puppy 1 jumps up on a chair that is even with a recycling bin.
- 🐾 Puppy 1 jumps into the bin.
- 🐾 Puppy 2 spies a leather glove atop a pile of firewood against the tent wall.
- 🐾 Puppy 2 climbs up the pile of firewood and snatches the glove.
- 🐾 The pile of firewood comes tumbling down as Puppy 2 leaps clear.
- 🐾 Puppy 1 pops out of the bin with a paper bag in her jaws.
- 🐾 Puppy 1 proceeds to wrestle with the bag as if she had caught a delicious salmon.
- 🐾 Puppy 3 sees what Puppy 1 is doing and joins in the fun.

- 🐾 Puppy 3 noodles around in the bin and comes out with an empty glass bottle.
- 🐾 Puppy 3 plays soccer with the bottle, which rolls, spins, and skids across the flooring.
- 🐾 Puppy 4 latches on to the glove in Puppy 2's mouth and begins a tug-of-war.

Sounds of a pup playground fill the air: growling, ripping, rolling, banging, snarling, and whining. The noise was like a joyful symphony to us, though others might describe it as a train wreck.

Even feeding time could be a raucous event. As I would climb into their pen with two warm baby bottles of formula, I would ask the pups, "Who's first? Is everybody first?" Then I would sit on the floor and cradle a pup in one arm while holding a bottle up to its mouth with my other arm. I'd barely get into position before another impatient pup would tackle my arm holding the bottle, grasp the nipple, and suck with a force that almost yanked the bottle from my hand.

At the same time, the first pup would try to grab the bottle from the second pup with its forelimbs while pushing against my stomach with it hind limbs. In a flurry of flailing limbs and frantically whining pups, I somehow managed to balance the little fur balls long enough for them to eat.

After playtime and mealtime, with bodies weary and stomachs full, the pups would curl up in our laps and take a well-needed snooze. I think these were the moments when we really connected with the young wolves. As they lay in our laps, wrapped in warm blankets, a trusting relationship took root. They bonded with us and we bonded with them.

We always avoided treating the wolves as pets, and that included the pups. However, we still decided to name them. It was simply a convenient way to distinguish one wolf from another.

If this was a purely scientific study, we might have just assigned each wolf a number. But this wasn't a scientific study. It was a project to experience wolves as no one ever had, by living with them, and to share not only what we observed and learned but also what we felt. Names, rather than numbers, would help us connect with the wolves on a more personal level, and they were certainly more interesting.

So, what to call them?

We decided to give them Native American names, as we had done with the adult wolves, since the wolf was an important part of Native American culture, and both had once lived freely across the land. It was fun looking through dictionaries of the Blackfoot and Lakota languages to find names that had a beautiful sound as well as a special meaning.

Two of the puppies were brothers. They looked like identical twins, with the classic gray, white, and black markings of a gray wolf. We named one Kamots (KAH-mots), Blackfoot for "freedom." He was the most adventurous of the pups and seemed impatient to get out of his pen and explore the outside world.

His brother was a sweet and playful pup we named Lakota (la-COAT-ah). That's the Lakota word for "friend."

Their sister had black fur and was the most vocal of the four. We named her Aipuyi (eye-POO-ee), which means "one who speaks a lot" in the Blackfoot language.

The fourth pup was unrelated to the other three. She had a dark coat of black and brown and a personality that was shy and mysterious. The Blackfoot word for "shadow" seemed fitting, so we named her Motaki (ma-TAH-kee).

The wolves never knew their names. We never called to them, as one would do with a pet. They were wild, and wild they would stay. Everything was on their terms, and we didn't interfere as they communicated with one another and sorted out their puppy hierarchy.

Outside the cook tent became the pups' introduction to the great outdoors, but I didn't just let them loose. I fenced off a small area so they could get used to the natural world and be safe. Nights were still spent inside, and even outside during the day someone was with the pups at all times. We were always concerned that a coyote or even an owl might grab them.

The puppies loved being outside. They sniffed the fresh air. They rolled in the soft grass. They nibbled on the flowers and gnawed on branches.

Mostly they played.

Every stick was a toy to be picked up, dragged around, and chewed. Chewing was the main way the puppies satisfied their curiosity about objects, whether it be a stick, a shoe, a finger, or an expensive camera. Many of my cameras still bear the scratch marks of puppy playtime, and I think every member of the crew sacrificed at least one article of clothing to those tiny sharp teeth.

The pups grew quickly, adding about three pounds (1.4 kg) each week. They became stronger and stronger. After a few weeks, when they were large enough to spend some time unsupervised, we moved them to a fenced-off area near the main enclosure. This puppy enclosure was only about the size of a baseball diamond but included a creek, trees, and open fields—plenty for wolf pups to explore.

And explore they did.

Kamots led the way. He was the most alert and curious of the pups. If a rustling came from the willows, Kamots trotted toward the sound to investigate while the others held back.

Courageous and confident, Kamots was up for any challenge. The trunk of a fallen tree might look too difficult for the others to climb on, but Kamots would find a way. He might hop onto a branch, reach for the main trunk, and pull himself aboard. The next thing you knew, he was stepping along the trunk like a gymnast on a balance beam.

The Sawtooth pups stayed in their enclosure throughout July. The adults gazed at them across the grassy strip that separated the enclosures and howled with excitement. The pups answered with howls of their own, though they sounded more like high-pitched yelps and yodels.

I remember holding Kamots in my arms as a howl from one of the adults caught his attention. He threw back his head and let out one puppy howl after another with all the strength he could muster. He seemed so confident, I wondered if he would eventually become the leader of the pack.

By August, the pups were 14 weeks old. They had bonded with us and were ready to meet the adult wolves.

This was a key moment in the project. So far everything had gone as well as I could've hoped. I had located a site, secured permits, built the enclosure, adopted wolves, and bonded with the pups. But if the adults didn't accept the pups, there would be no pack, and the project would fall apart.

I needed to talk to a friend who understood the meaning of this moment. I called Jamie.

I told her about my plan to introduce the wolves slowly. I would show the pups to the adults through the fence. If that went well, I'd release the pups into the enclosure the following day.

I was nervous. But Jamie reminded me that my friend in Germany agreed with my plan and was certain the adults would welcome the pups. I felt better, as I always did after hearing Jamie's voice.

The next day we brought the pups up to the fence. I crouched down with Kamots in my arms. Akai approached to meet this little stranger whose yodeling had fascinated him for weeks. Kamots became very excited and squirmed in my arms. He wanted to meet his new foster parents.

At the same time, Akai started whining and pacing the fence. I could see he was upset, and I understood why. Akai thought I might harm Kamots and the other pups, and he was looking for a way to get through the fence to protect them. Akai and Makuyi had not grown up with us and did not trust us the way the pups did. I was impressed by Akai's protective instincts.

On the other hand, Makuyi's reaction to the pups surprised me. She was interested in them, but she didn't come up to the fence to greet them. She held back. I wondered how she would react when they were all together.

I found out early the next morning.

We placed the pups in the lock-off area for a few minutes to let all the wolves get familiar with the new sights, sounds, and smells. For the first time, Makuyi approached the pups and sniffed each one through the fencing. I was relieved that she was finally meeting them.

The pups wanted in. They whined and wagged their tails furiously as they jumped over each other, stood on their hind legs, and pawed at the fence. The anticipation grew. Then we opened the gate.

The pups hesitated for just a split second. Then with a burst of energy, they charged toward Akai. They pushed and squeezed their way past one another to reach his muzzle with licks of greeting. Akai in turn licked the pups on the face and head. Tails wagged in excitement. The pups then rolled over on their backs, showing that they recognized Akai as the dominant wolf.

The pups followed Akai as he trotted off to show them their new home. It was the happy scene I had hoped for, and I was thrilled to capture it all on film. The wolves were now together as a family, as a wolf pack.

But something was wrong.

As I watched the pups with Akai, I realized that Makuyi was nowhere in sight. A crew member said that she ran off as soon as the pups had charged in. I had no idea why she was avoiding them, but it seemed that wolf behavior was more complex than I thought. I also didn't know where she went. Was she hiding, or had something happened to her?

We had to find Makuyi. 🐾

## CHAPTER 4

# TROUBLE
# IN THE PACK

## JIM

We started our search for Makuyi immediately. First, we checked the perimeter to make sure there were no breaks in the fence through which she could have escaped. All was secure.

Next, we swept through the interior of the enclosure. We looked everywhere, from the creek that ran through the willows and aspens, to the ponds among the firs, to the distant pine forests, and every meadow in between.

There was no sign of her. Not on the first day, not on the second day. *She must be hiding somewhere*, I thought, *but where?*

As a wild animal, if Makuyi didn't want to be found, she probably wouldn't be. I figured our best chance of success was if we happened to see her moving from one hiding place to another, perhaps from behind a downed tree to a thicket of willows. I only hoped she wasn't lying hurt somewhere.

Finally, on the third day of searching, I found a hole several feet deep. I knelt and peered into it, wondering if I might see Makuyi peering back. I didn't.

I looked up at my search partner, who was pointing toward a distant hillside. I followed his gaze and saw Makuyi's tan-and-gray coat glistening in the midday sun as she trotted across a meadow.

"There she is!"

I felt instant relief. But the question remained: Why was she avoiding Akai and the pups? I still didn't know the answer.

As I watched Makuyi disappear into the trees, my relief turned to deep sadness. She was heading off to spend the rest of the day and night by herself yet again. I could sense how lonely she was, like a stranger in her own pack—in her own family.

Over the next several weeks, she periodically came out of hiding and approached the rest of the pack timidly, as if to "test the waters" of acceptance. But by then, the other wolves wanted nothing to do with her. They chased her off, and she appeared too afraid to stand up to them.

I felt so sorry for Makuyi. I wished there was something I could do to help her.

As it turned out, there was, and as one might expect with wolves, it centered around food. One day, my crew and I brought the pack a deer that had been hit and killed by a vehicle on the road. Just like with the cougar project, such roadkill was the Sawtooth Pack's main source of food. In the wild, a wolf pack might roam its territory for days in search of large prey, such as a deer or elk. The pack chases and brings down the prey, then consumes just about every scrap of meat the animal provides. The wolves then rest for several days and digest the meal before searching for food again. I mimicked this pattern as much as I could by bringing in a large roadkill every five days or so.

We first lured the pack into the lock-off. Then we carried the deer into the enclosure, laid it in a clearing, stepped away, and radioed a crew member to release the wolves.

As usual, the mere presence of food stirred excitement within the pack. The wolves quickly approached the carcass, bustling about and jockeying for position around it. As they did, young Kamots asserted himself, growling and snapping at the others, including Akai.

I wasn't surprised at this behavior. It's a natural part of wolf language that I felt was so misunderstood. In a wolf pack, the highest ranking member—the leader of the pack—eats first. And Kamots appeared to be stepping into a new role as leader.

It wasn't always so.

When the pups first joined the pack in the summer, Akai was the undisputed head of the newly formed family. The youngsters held their head lower than his. They greeted him each morning with lots of licks and wagging tails. They followed him on explorations and ate whatever he ate.

Soon, however, things began to change. A new leader was emerging.

Kamots had always been confident and brave. These qualities grew as he did. Week after week I noticed Kamots following less and leading more. He often was the first one to trot up and greet me each day when I entered their territory to film. He struck off on his own to investigate new sounds instead of waiting for Akai. He also was becoming more dominant during pack rallies, positioning himself higher than Akai while howling.

By late fall, it was clear that Kamots was taking control of the pack, and no wolf, not even the older and bigger Akai, challenged him. Among other things, that meant Kamots presided at mealtime.

Kamots kept a watchful eye on the rest of the pack as he tore into the deer carcass. When another wolf tried to sneak a nibble, Kamots stopped chewing and growled, as if to say "Back off." Only when Kamots was well into his meal did he allow the other wolves to eat.

All except Makuyi, that is. The pack didn't allow her to eat with them at all. If she tried, the pack drove her away.

On this particular day, Makuyi appeared out of the woods across the meadow and watched the rest of the pack eat their fill. She looked so thin and hungry. I figured she was catching rabbits, mice, and other small prey, but that would not be enough.

So, I had come up with a plan: I would smuggle food to her.

I had to be sneaky about it. The other wolves would harass Makuyi mercilessly if they knew I was bringing her food. Fortunately, after the wolves had gorged themselves, they wanted to do nothing but lie around. That's when I acted.

I stuffed my backpack with chunks of deer meat that I had put aside from the carcass that we had fed the pack. I circled around the enclosure far from the fence line so that the pack would not see me.

Entering through a distant gate at the top end of their territory, completely out of sight of the other wolves, I hiked to the clearing where I often saw Makuyi. I placed the meat on the ground, then sat back and waited ... and watched ...

She was hiding out there somewhere, watching me. She was afraid but also hungry, and I hoped her hunger would bring her out of hiding. It did.

After half an hour, she timidly stepped out from a grove of spruce trees but would not approach the food until I left. Then she gobbled it up with such gusto that I wished I'd brought more.

I continued smuggling food to Makuyi daily in hopes of not only keeping up her strength but gaining her trust. I had a feeling that if I could get near her, I could understand more about her problem and help her. But first she had to trust me, and that would take time.

Finally, as winter snows laid a blanket of white over the Sawtooth Mountains, Makuyi found the courage to approach me. I placed a deer leg on the ground and plunked myself down in the snow nearby.

Makuyi emerged from the willows as usual, but this time came forward. She circled slowly at a distance and then crept toward the food. As she did, I noticed a damp spot on her left side. The fur there was darker and matted, and I thought, *Did she lie in tree sap?*

As she crept a little closer, I saw the alarming answer. The damp spot was blood! Clearly one of the other wolves had bitten her.

In the next instant Makuyi snatched the meat and ran off with it into the willows. I walked back to my tent that day with a heavy heart.

As January turned to February, I made slow but steady progress in gaining Makuyi's trust. Each week I sat closer and closer to the food. Then one day I held a chunk of meat in my outstretched hand and waited for her to take the food from me. She did—then promptly ran off with it.

From that time on, she started to become relaxed and comfortable around me. Her fear subsided, and soon we visited even when I didn't bring food. We sat near each other in the snow. I talked softly and soothingly to her. One day after she ate, she walked over to me and licked my hand. Then she sat down and looked at me with those auburn eyes of hers.

I had finally gained Makuyi's trust.

I was happy, of course, but also sad because I realized that I was her only friend. That realization hit me hard one bitterly cold February evening.

I had just returned on my snowmobile from the town of Stanley, where I had picked up some supplies. I had had trouble starting the vehicle in Stanley, so I was very late getting back to camp. By the time I did, it was too late to enter the enclosure, so I couldn't visit Makuyi. Our rule was that the nights belonged to the wolves, so we never entered their territory after dark.

The engine and headlights of the snowmobile announced my return, and the pack rushed to the fence to greet me. As they took turns licking my hand through the chain-link, a faint howl rose up from a distant pine forest.

It was Makuyi. Her howl was like a long, mournful cry.

Typically, the rest of the pack would return the howl. Not this time. They remained silent. They ignored her. The wolves weren't being mean; they perhaps were just showing that they didn't consider Makuyi a member of the pack. I knew this, but still it broke my heart to think of how lonely she must have felt. I put myself in her place and I ached for her.

Though I understood her loneliness, I still didn't understand why she had become a loner. Wolves are extremely social animals. Like people, they need one another. Just as a person identifies with his or her family, a wolf identifies with his or her pack. A human family has parents, grandparents, brothers, sisters, aunts, and uncles, most born into the family but some adopted into it. So does a wolf pack.

Like other mistaken notions about wolves, the idea of a "lone wolf" is largely legend. About the only time a wolf chooses to be alone is when he or she leaves the pack to look for a mate and start a new pack. These wolves are called dispersers. Wolves need to have a bond with one another and be part of something larger than themselves—they need to be part of a pack.

Which is why Makuyi's situation didn't add up. Though she was literally crying out to bond with the others, I was baffled as to why she chose to run and hide in the first place.

Then I discovered the answer.

While filming her up close, I noticed that her eyes were clouded over. On the first day I had met her in Montana, I learned from Karin that she might have cataracts. If she did, the condition must have become much worse over the past months. She seemed nearly blind.

Now it all made sense. She probably had been uncertain and afraid of the new pups because she could barely see them. I also had noticed that she hid in the same few spots and followed the same few trails through the snow. Of course! She was using familiar trails that she had memorized and could follow by scent.

I had to do something to help prevent Makuyi from going completely blind. That meant finding a medical expert. I knew the one person who could help me. I called Jamie.

Jamie had been helping to treat and care for all kinds of animals, including wolves, at the National Zoo hospital. Her experience—and her common sense—had helped guide me from before the project began, and I needed that guidance now more than ever. I also needed to reach out to a friend.

I was glad I did.

Jamie suggested I contact a local veterinarian to find a veterinary ophthalmologist. She said these eye specialists had successfully performed cataract surgery on dogs, and there was no reason to think it wouldn't work on a wolf.

As we talked, I felt my burden easing. I became hopeful that surgery could restore Makuyi's eyesight, which would give her confidence and perhaps a place in the pack. By the time I hung up the phone, I knew the way forward.

As Jamie had figured, a veterinarian was able to put me in touch with a top-notch animal eye surgeon. He was from Portland, Oregon, and transporting Makuyi would be too stressful for her, so the surgeon flew out to wolf camp. He brought crates of medical equipment and we rented a portable generator for electricity. The yurt shifted from a kitchen to an operating room.

With camp set up as a field hospital, I met Makuyi in her usual hiding place. I hid a mild sedative in some meat, which she gobbled up, and then further sedated her with an injection before carrying her into the yurt on a stretcher.

First, the surgeon stitched up wounds that had been inflicted on her by the other wolves. I gently stroked the fur of her ear and reassured her, "It's going to be okay, Makuyi. It's going to be okay."

After stitching the wounds, the surgeon operated on her right eye, which was totally blind. He removed Makuyi's cornea and replaced it with a synthetic one. We decided to leave the other eye alone to reduce risk during the operation.

Nearly four hours later, the surgery was complete. As the anesthetic wore off, Makuyi was able to stand on wobbly legs. She stepped forward with confidence.

She could see!

I was elated. But would Makuyi's restored sight make her more acceptable to the pack? There was only one way to find out—by releasing her into the enclosure.

But first I had to make sure that the scent Makuyi carried from the operating room would not be so foreign to the rest of the pack that they would attack her. So I covered rags with antiseptic and Makuyi's blood and gave them to the wolves. They sniffed the rags and rolled around in them. Soon they all smelled like Makuyi ... at least, I hoped they did.

As Makuyi entered the enclosure, the pups, now almost a year old, ignored her. Akai approached her and inspected her, giving a few curious sniffs but no welcoming licks. That night I told my crew, "Well, it wasn't the homecoming I was hoping for, but at least she wasn't attacked."

I spoke too soon.

The next morning, Makuyi was not with the rest of the pack. Alarmed, we searched through the enclosure, including her main hiding place among some spruce trees, but she wasn't there. As we headed back to where the pack hung out, we found her lying still among the willows. The snow was stained with blood from numerous fresh wounds.

"Oh, no!" I gasped.

We scooped her up onto a stretcher as quickly and as gently as we could and carried her out of the enclosure.

The other wolves had been put in the lock-off area until we were out of the gate. As I passed, I looked at them all and wondered which one had carried out this vicious attack. I never found out for sure, but my guess was Aipuyi. She was quick-tempered and could be aggressive.

I was saddened and worried, but I wasn't angry, not with Aipuyi or any other wolf. I was learning that aggression, fear, and jealousy were as much a part of a pack's hidden life as kindness, compassion, and care. They were all a natural part of the complex bag of wolf pack behaviors. Not that different from humans, really.

In this case, though, I couldn't let nature take its course. I had brought the pack together, so I felt responsible for doing everything I could to keep the wolves healthy. We took Makuyi straight to the yurt. The surgeon was still in camp, and he tended to her wounds.

When she was all stitched up, we wrapped her in blankets and took her back to my house in Ketchum. While a crew member stayed with the pack, Makuyi stayed in a large pen in my garage on soft, comfortable pads for two weeks. I changed her dressings, hand-fed her, and even slept beside her to keep her company. I wasn't sure she would live.

Choking back tears, I called Jamie to let her know what happened. I knew she would understand and care. As it turned out, we depended on each other for such understanding, for a month later, Jamie called me in tears with a tragic story of how Rufus, the kangaroo she had been raising, had suddenly died. With setbacks like these, it was nice for each of us to hear a comforting voice.

One night, while sleeping next to Makuyi, I awoke and saw her huge silhouette looming over me. I stared up at her reddish brown eyes staring down. She was standing for the first time since being attacked!

From that moment, she improved quickly and started showing more typical wolf behavior ... like urinating on my sleeping pad. I didn't mind too much. It was a sign of a healthy wolf—she was simply marking the item as her own. She once again became the sweet and confident animal that I had first seen at the shelter in Montana.

Clearly that was the place to which she now had to return. She couldn't go back to the Sawtooth Pack. She was an outsider there. Thankfully her old pack at the wolf shelter still remembered her and welcomed her back.

As I watched her greet old friends, I felt relief but also gratitude. I was grateful to Makuyi. She had been patient with me, and I with her. We had given each other time to learn. She taught me how wolves need to be with other wolves. It's all about family.

In spite of the hardships she endured, she could now see, and I knew in my heart that she forgave me. I was most grateful for that.

Though Makuyi was gone, trouble remained, and Akai was its name.

Akai wasn't a bad wolf. Quite the opposite—he was protective of the younger ones, who were now a year old and called yearlings.

The problem was that Akai had not grown up with my crew or me. Even though he was habituated to people, he wasn't habituated to *us*.

This created a situation that wasn't safe for him or my crew. The yearlings, on the other hand, trusted us completely. To them we were each a foster parent and friend.

Whenever I entered the enclosure, the youngsters ran up to greet me, which seemed to bewilder and aggravate Akai. He began to place himself between the yearlings and me. I was concerned with this behavior at first but not alarmed. Then things started to get out of hand.

Whenever I approached the enclosure, Akai would follow me from the other side, snap at the fence, and growl menacingly. I became concerned each time I entered.

One day I was in the enclosure with my researcher taking photos of the pack. Akai wanted us out. I could hear his deep, low, continuous growl, like distant thunder rumbling across the sky. The situation was becoming too dangerous and we decided to leave.

As we opened the gate, our backs to Akai, he attacked.

I heard his paws pounding the ground and I swung around just as he jumped on me. I held the camera tripod in front of me for some protection, but Akai reached around it and bit my forearm.

A wolf's bite is strong enough to crush bone, but Akai didn't clamp down with all his might. He was only sending a warning: "Stay away from the yearlings!" Still, even his warning had enough force to pierce my jacket and break through my skin.

The last straw came a month later when he suddenly turned on my researcher. Akai had her pinned against the fence and showed his teeth in a menacing growl whenever she tried to step away. I distracted Akai while she made a dash for the gate. She got out safely, but we could no longer take such chances.

For the project to continue, all of the wolves had to trust us, and Akai clearly did not. I had to find him another home.

As luck would have it, I received a call from a wolf refuge in Colorado. They had a lone female and were hoping to find her a male companion. I thought, *Have I got a wolf for you!* We helped finance the construction of an enclosure big enough for two wolves, and then flew Akai to his new home, where the pair lived together happily for many years.

The Sawtooth Pack was now down to the four yearlings. Kamots was the clear leader of the puppy pack—the alpha wolf. Motaki was the lowest ranking member—the omega wolf. Aipuyi and Lakota jockeyed for position in the middle of the pack.

But change was coming.

Winter had finally released its icy grip and the Idaho Rockies welcomed the warmth of spring. Snowmelt swelled the creek, which ran cold and deep. Wildflowers once again dotted the meadows and carpeted the forests in splashes of blue, red, and yellow.

And as the wolf project entered its second year, three new pups were getting ready to join the pack. This was the best change of all. 🐾

## CHAPTER 5

# SEASON OF CHANGE

## JIM

Once again, our camp became a nursery for some very rambunctious wolf pups. This time there were three, all brothers. We received them from the same Montana wolf shelter that provided us with the first four pups.

Though part of the same litter, the brothers looked as different as wolves could possibly look, ranging from black to gray to beige. We gave them Blackfoot names. As the pups grew, we were to discover that sometimes the names fit their personalities and sometimes they didn't.

Motomo (muh-TOE-moe), or "he who goes first," was jet-black with a splash of white on his chest. Of all the wolves, he was the most curious about people. He could sit for hours just watching me film or do chores.

Amani (uh-MA-knee), or "speaks the truth," had the classic gray coat with black and white markings, like Kamots and Lakota. If there were a Blackfoot word for "class clown," it would've been a more fitting name for Amani. He was always acting silly, like the time he suddenly plopped over on his side as I walked by, just to get attention.

Matsi (MOT-zee), or "sweet and brave," on the other hand, fit his name to a T. This spirited blond pup would grow up to be my favorite wolf of all.

Many times I'd sit next to the fence while bottle-feeding one of the pups. The pack would crowd on the other side and whine with excitement.

Much like humans, youngsters often bring out the best in adults. It always struck me as incredibly sweet how the adult wolves took an interest in the pups, and how concerned they were. I'd lift a puppy to the fence and let an adult lick him on the nose. Then the pup would turn back to me and lick *my* nose. It was a very special and wonderful bonding experience.

After the troubles with Makuyi and Akai, it felt like the Sawtooth Pack was finally hitting its stride. Spring was turning to summer and the warmth of the seasons seemed to promise bright days ahead.

Little did I know that tragedy was lurking right around the corner.

The phone rang as I walked into my house.

It was a rainy evening in June, and I was spending the night in Ketchum charging camera batteries and resupplying camp. I picked up the phone, wondering who could be calling at this time of night.

It was a member of my crew, and she had a troubling report. A deer carcass had been placed in the enclosure for the wolves, and Motaki, one of the yearlings, had not shown up for the feeding. She never missed a meal, so I was deeply concerned. It was too dark to do anything then and there, except worry, but I left at dawn the next morning and sped back to wolf camp to begin the search.

We started by walking the perimeter to look for holes in the fence or a downed tree that could have been used as a ladder to scale the fence.

All was well with the fence line. But then, where was Motaki? Was she hiding? That didn't make sense. Unlike Makuyi, Motaki was accepted by the pack as a true member. Something had to be wrong to keep her from eating with the others. I thought she must be injured—or worse.

It was worse.

I found her body in a grove of aspens. The gentlest, most playful member of the pack was dead.

I couldn't believe what I was seeing. My most horrible nightmare had come to pass. *How could this have happened?* I asked myself over and over.

Then I realized Motaki must have wandered from the pack and been alone long enough for the killer to do this grizzly deed. Whether that killer was human or animal I did not know, but for a moment I feared the threat might still be nearby ... watching me ... I turned around slowly and peered deep into the forest. Every rustling leaf, every snapping twig drew my attention.

Detecting no immediate danger, I called my crew over and we scoured the ground for animal tracks, footprints—anything that would provide a clue about what had happened. We found nothing. I expected as much. The rain of the previous evening would have washed out any such evidence.

I resigned myself that Motaki's death would remain a mystery.

I slept restlessly that night. I kept picturing Motaki's body. A frightful gash tore open her belly. I knew I had seen that kind of wound before, but I couldn't place it. What was I missing?

Suddenly I remembered another detail that almost made me bolt right out of my cot. The area around the gash had been cleaned of fur. My mind flashed back to the cougar I had filmed a few years before. When I left her a carcass, she always licked the fur off the belly of her prey with her sandpaper-like tongue before she ate it.

Now I knew what to look for near Motaki's body.

The next morning I returned to the site and searched for signs of a cougar attack. It didn't take long to find clues.

A patch of black wolf fur was snagged on the bark of a nearby aspen tree about seven feet (2 m) high on a large branch. A little below that were several claw marks, not from a cougar but from wolves. Above the patch of black wolf fur were numerous thin scratches, just like the ones made by a cougar's razor-sharp claws.

I began to create a horrific picture in my mind of what most likely happened.

A cougar had climbed a tree next to the fence and jumped into the enclosure. Did the cougar, perhaps traveling through its territory, first see Motaki from outside the fence, or only after it was already inside? I had no way of knowing.

However, one thing was clear: The attack occurred when Motaki was alone. A cougar would never go up against a pack of wolves, but one-on-one, a wolf doesn't stand a chance. Motaki's strength, teeth, and other defenses were no match for the big cat's immense power and lightning speed. Undoubtedly the kill was swift.

But why was there wolf fur so high up in the tree? The other wolves probably heard a yelp and ran to investigate. The cougar, sensing danger from the pack, must have then dragged Motaki's body into the tree, as these big cats are known to do with their prey.

There was no direct evidence as to how the cougar escaped the wolves, but I could easily picture a powerful, agile cougar jumping down from the tree, outrunning the pack, and scaling the fence. During the frantic getaway, poor Motaki's body must have fallen back to the ground.

That scenario made sense, but I began to ponder others. Maybe after growling at the pack and jumping out of the tree, the cougar evaded the wolves and hid within the enclosure ...

I drew in a sharp breath. *What if the cougar was still somewhere within the fence line?*

That frightening possibility sent chills down my spine. I imagined the silent predator stalking the remaining wolves, and perhaps us, waiting for the right moment to strike. It was highly unlikely, but then, so was Motaki's death. I wasn't about to take a chance. I called the crew together and we searched the enclosure high and low. We found no other trace of the big cat, but I remained anxious for months.

The attack on Motaki was a grim reminder that the Sawtooth Pack could not be protected from every danger. Even though the area was fenced off, Meadow Creek was still wild, and wilderness holds dangers for all animals as they struggle to survive.

I knew there was nothing I could've done to prevent Motaki's tragic death, but it didn't lessen the pain in my heart. I ached over the loss of this gentle wolf.

The sadness of the pack seemed even greater and more personal than my own. I lost a friend, but they lost a member of their family. They lost a part of themselves.

The wolves no longer played. Anyone who watched the pack in happier times would understand how unusual that was.

Play is an important part of a wolf's day, and in the Sawtooth Pack, Motaki had been the instigator. She could always get the pack in a playful mood. She might approach a wolf and drop into a "play bow," in which she quickly lowered the front part of her body, spread her forelimbs wide, and wagged her tail, daring the other wolf to chase her. More often than not, the dare was accepted and the chase was on. Soon all the wolves in the pack would be chasing one another in a session of good-natured tag.

But now that Motaki was gone, the other wolves weren't interested. They seemed too sad to play, and they didn't for the next six weeks.

Not only could I see the pack's sadness, I also could hear it. Usually when the wolves howled, they did so as a group. They would throw back their heads and sing out in a loud chorus. Their howls were a joyful celebration of pack life.

After Motaki's death, each wolf howled alone. The sounds now seemed like cries of mourning. They had an eerie searching quality to them, as if the wolves were trying to call Motaki back.

The wolves were indeed mourning, and they were depressed. The changes in their behavior left no doubt in my mind.

Over the next few weeks, every time I went walking among the aspens where we had found Motaki the pack followed close behind. As the wolves passed over the exact spot where Motaki's body had been, they sniffed the ground.

That didn't surprise me, but as they sniffed, they pinned back their ears and lowered their tails. This gesture is normally used only when a wolf submits to another, recognizing its higher status. Motaki was the omega—the lowest ranking wolf in the pack. In life, no pack mate would have dared pay her such respect. In death, they all did. It was a touching tribute.

Motaki's death was a devastating blow to the Sawtooth Pack and to everyone involved in the project. For six weeks the wolves wandered the enclosure aimlessly. In a way, so did I. Was the project worth this agony? I began to wonder ...

Ultimately, I realized that I could not control all of the tragic events that might befall the pack. The struggle to survive is part of life in the natural world. I understood that. We all did.

Still, it was a painful time.

The pack's behavior eventually returned to normal. And though I always carried Motaki's memory with me, the crew and I snapped out of our funk, too.

Fortunately, Motomo, Amani, and Matsi were waiting in the wings to lift everyone's spirits.

Shortly after Motaki's death, the second class of pups graduated from a pen in our tent to the puppy enclosure outside. And later that summer, at the age of 12 weeks, they joined the young adults, Kamots, Lakota, and Aipuyi.

I was glad to see that this time every adult welcomed the newcomers. After several minutes of warm greetings, Kamots led the pups on a tour of their new home.

As I watched "Sawtooth Pack 2.0" trot off into the pines, I wondered how their six personalities would sort out. Pups hold special status in a pack. They can get away with things that others can't, like climbing all over the adults at playtime and being first in line at mealtime. But as the months pass, the pups must compete for a position in the adult hierarchy. What role would each wolf play? Would anyone challenge Kamots as the alpha? Who would take Motaki's place as the omega?

I hadn't yet fully appreciated the significance of these roles. In the coming year, the wolves themselves would show me what it truly means to be an alpha and an omega. They would reveal more about their hidden lives than ever before, including some surprises that were sweet and some that were shocking. 🐾

## CHAPTER 6

# A COMPASSIONATE ALPHA

## JIM

Kamots charged through the meadow at full speed. With each powerful stride, he kicked up a powdery spray of white. It reminded me of the dust trail that follows my van as I barrel down a dry dirt road, except what was kicked up from his paws wasn't dirt but snow.

It was the first big snowfall of the year and Kamots was loving it. Falling snow almost always made the wolves happy and playful. On this snowy day, Kamots was jubilant. I could barely keep up with him as I filmed his antics. He ran in circles, then darted off in one direction and zigzagged in others.

Kamots got Amani's attention, too. Amani had been enjoying his first snowfall at wolf camp, but for the moment, he simply sat and watched Kamots, mesmerized by the pack leader's sudden burst of energy.

At one point, Kamots disappeared into the willows. A moment later he shot out of the dense thicket like a rocket and plowed right over Amani. The young wolf did a somersault and ended up back in the sitting position, covered in snow. He blinked away the powder from his eyes. He had that confused look on his face that said, "What just happened?"

That's when Kamots showed me how wolves care.

Realizing what he had done, he slammed on the brakes and rushed back to Amani. Kamots looked Amani over and sniffed him to make sure he was uninjured. He then gave the young wolf a few comforting licks, as if to apologize for his carelessness.

I thought to myself, *This is a true alpha.*

Every wolf has a social position in its pack. Each position helps keep order and harmony, which in turn helps the wolves live together and survive in the wild. The top position is the pack leader—the alpha.

From the time Kamots was a very young pup, I felt that someday he might be the alpha of the Sawtooth Pack. It was evident even at two weeks old. That's when we separated one pup at a time from the rest of the litter for bottle-feeding.

Not all pups responded the same. When we removed Aipuyi, she became nervous and trembled in fear. She didn't want to roam around; she only wanted to get back to her siblings. It was like she felt that if she was away too long, she would lose her social position in the puppy hierarchy.

Kamots's reaction was completely different. When we removed him from the litter, he took the opportunity to explore. He sniffed each human caretaker and then inspected every object he could find.

Here was a wolf that enjoyed new experiences! Kamots was curious, calm, and confident.

As Kamots grew, so did his confidence. He showed leadership in everything he did. Whether walking or standing, he held his tail and head higher than the rest of the pack. When I entered the wolves' territory, he would be the first to greet me.

Kamots was always on the lookout for threats and alert to anything out of the ordinary. When an unusual sound rang out from the forest, he was the one that trotted off to investigate. No doubt he was first to reach the tree in which Makuyi's attacker took refuge, and I'm quite certain the highest claw marks on that aspen trunk belonged to the courageous Kamots.

Though a brave protector and kind leader, Kamots made it clear that his position and authority were not to be challenged, including at mealtime.

Kamots often allowed the pups, Amani, Motomo, and Matsi, to join him in eating from a carcass first, but he did not extend this privilege to the other adults.

One day as I was filming, Lakota, who had now taken on the social position as omega, dared to approach an elk carcass and eat before his turn. He slunk toward the carcass across from Kamots, keeping low and moving slow, as if trying to sneak a bite without anyone noticing.

Not a chance. Kamots raised his eyes toward Lakota, bared his teeth, and let out a low, rumbling growl. That was a friendly warning.

Lakota understood, but he was hungry, and he continued ever so slowly toward the tempting meal.

Kamots suddenly became furious. His facial features changed dramatically. He raised his lips to fully expose his teeth. At the same time he scrunched up his nose, which wrinkled and widened his muzzle, making him look ferocious. When he stuck his ears straight out like horns, the transformation was complete. He looked like a totally different wolf—a snarling, fearsome beast that meant business.

Before Lakota could react to this new set of ominous warnings, Kamots leaped over the elk toward his brother. This time Lakota got the message. He ran a few steps, flopped over on his back, and let out a sharp *yelp!* That's wolf for, "Okay, okay, I give up!"

As tough as Kamots could be, he was never vicious. He didn't actually hurt Lakota, and after he made his point, he returned to his usual calm self. He never held a grudge.

One sunny day in late fall, in the third year of the project, I entered the enclosure without my camera just to watch the wolves and think. I sat on a hill overlooking the meadow as the pack played together below.

So many changes had taken place over the past three years, and there was a lot to think about. Makuyi had been rejected by the pack, Akai had been removed after becoming a threat to the crew, and Motaki had been killed by a cougar.

Of course, there were happy changes, too. Kamots was becoming a confident and caring alpha, while Lakota, Matsi, Amani, and Motomo had settled into their roles. Our film would soon be finished, and it would clearly illustrate how amazing wolves are.

I was touched by the pack's reaction to Motaki's death. Obviously, these wolves were a lot more devoted to one another than I had first thought. I was beginning to understand that a pack was more than a group of wolves that had banded together. A pack was a family and they cared about one another.

Still, not everyone shared our feelings about wolves, and they wanted the project to end. Such attitudes as well as recent events had tested my confidence to continue.

We would often receive threatening letters in the mail, and at one point a sign appeared near our camp saying, "Move the wolves or we will." This was very upsetting, but my underlying fear was that the Forest Service might eventually feel the pressure to cancel our land-use permits.

There was also my concern about Aipuyi, one of our mid-ranking pack members. She was becoming more and more aggressive with the other wolves, and I worried how she might affect the stability of the entire pack. What difficulties lay ahead there? I had no idea.

Something else was troubling me. As the editing of our film was approaching completion, I felt that I was missing the most important part of the wolves' story. As Kamots and his family were maturing, they were clearly telling me something I hadn't put into the film. They were showing me how family oriented they were, how they cared for one another. I was missing a chance to tell that part of their story, and it troubled me.

Maybe I needed to make a second film to capture what I had missed in the first …

While I pondered where the project had been and where it was going, I suddenly felt terribly alone. I thought of Jamie and how we had once fleshed out sequences for my cougar film over meals together in Washington. More than anything, I wished she were here. I needed her input and spirit. Most of all, I needed her friendship.

Then from the corner of my eye, I realized that I was being watched. Kamots had been sitting a few feet away, surveying what I might be up to. He walked over and licked my face. It was his usual greeting. But instead of trotting off like he normally did, he sat next to me, cocked his head, and gave me a look that seemed to say: "What's wrong?"

Kamots knew me so well.

Then he did something I had never experienced before. He raised his paw and stretched it toward me. Following his lead, I raised my hand to meet his paw, and we just sat there, hand to paw.

It was a moment I'll never forget.

Kamots's compassionate gesture meant the world to me. I felt his strength and calm, and at that moment, I knew everything was going to be all right. As long as I kept the project going, Kamots would take care of the rest. He would lead the pack to stability.

So, with my new vision of what a second wolf film might look like, a wishful dream about Jamie, and a nod from Kamots, I applied for an extension of our Forest Service permits.

Kamots had taken action that eased my troubles. In other words, all I can say is that I felt he had shown compassion. In the coming months, I would have to take action to ease the suffering of the entire pack. It, too, would be compassionate. It would also be devastating. 🐾

# CHAPTER 7

# A GUT-WRENCHING
# DECISION

## JIM

Aipuyi, the sister of Kamots and Lakota, had always been quick-tempered and unpredictable, even as a pup. As she grew, she became more and more of a tyrant. Her aggression wasn't directed at the crew or me; it was directed at the other wolves, mostly the yearling Motomo.

Motomo and Amani regularly had dominance fights, but they were harmless competitions and rarely drew blood. Motomo and Aipuyi drew blood.

Aipuyi was always the aggressor. She would just start attacking Motomo for no apparent reason, and the younger wolf was too stubborn to back down.

The battles became more intense and bloody in the late summer. If it continued much longer, I had no doubt Aipuyi eventually would kill Motomo, and perhaps other wolves after that.

I had to do something.

I immediately started contacting organizations that had captive wolves in hopes of finding Aipuyi another home. She couldn't join another pack, not with her aggressive behavior. Nor could I put her in a separate enclosure. Experts had assured me that isolating a wolf is torture to such a social animal.

My only hope was that someone out there had a lone male wolf. Then Aipuyi and the male could probably be companions and live together in peace.

As the months went by, no such organization or individual could be found. I was running out of options.

The violence increased continuously until everything came to a head one violent November afternoon during a pack rally.

As howls filled the crisp autumn air, I could see Aipuyi getting worked up. She became antsy and started challenging Motomo with nasty snarls. Motomo wasn't going to take it. He snarled back.

I had a bad feeling about this.

Suddenly in a violent burst, Aipuyi launched herself at him. Motomo leaped forward to meet rage with rage. Their bodies clashed and the fight was on.

Standing tall on their back legs, a blur of forelimbs beat the air and slapped against fur as each wolf tried to gain position. Aipuyi managed to grab hold of Motomo's neck and pull him downward, but the young wolf twisted out of it. He countered by driving her backward, trying to force her to the ground.

But Aipuyi maintained her balance. Then she jutted her muzzle forward, jaws open, fangs out for blood. Growling fiercely, she tried to clamp down on Motomo's neck, but with his lightning reflexes, she came away only with a few tufts of fur. They both dropped on all fours, where they continued to lunge, swipe, and snap at each other.

I had never seen such a frightening display of force and fury. I shouted, hoping to distract Aipuyi, but she battled with such rage, I doubt if a thunderbolt could have broken her focus. The other wolves didn't dare intervene in such a vicious fight, not even Kamots.

Then in a powerful move, Aipuyi flipped Motomo onto his back and bit deep into his thigh. He yelped in pain. Kicking wildly, Motomo escaped Aipuyi's hold and limped off into the willows. He could barely move one of his hind legs, and I feared he had severed a tendon.

Aipuyi lay down, exhausted. I could hear her heavy panting and see her body heaving with each quick breath. Several trickles of blood streamed down from bite wounds where Motomo had struck in self-defense.

I couldn't let this situation go on.

Aipuyi had become too dangerous and was threatening the well-being of the entire pack. So I made the decision that I had been contemplating and dreading for months. I called the veterinarian. The next day, I fed Aipuyi a mild sedative in a chunk of meat and then we took her out of the enclosure and quietly put her to sleep.

To this day, it is the most painful decision I have ever made. I had raised Aipuyi from a pup, and to end her life was gut-wrenching. Yet, there was no other choice. Every option had been exhausted.

One might ask, "Why didn't you just release her into the wild?" We couldn't have done that. First, it would have been illegal. But even if it were legal, it would be cruel and unethical. She would have been completely alone, and more than anything, a wolf needs to be part of a family, part of a pack.

In addition, Aipuyi lacked the one thing she needed to survive in the wild—a fear of humans. She would have stood perfectly still for a rancher or hunter pointing a rifle at her—she may have even approached the person. No wolf that is raised by people could ever survive in a land where human hunters roam.

In the end, I knew that the only choice I had was also the only compassionate one, not just for Aipuyi, but also for the entire pack. Still, I was overwhelmed with grief. I needed a compassionate voice. As usual, I found it in Jamie, along with healthy doses of wisdom, reassurance, and hope.

Over the phone, Jamie heard the despair in my voice as soon as I said "Hi." She knew that I had been trying desperately to find Aipuyi a home and to avoid what ultimately happened. Jamie understood exactly how I felt, and she shared my grief.

Then she assured me that I had made the right decision. In my heart I knew I had, but I needed to hear it from her, from someone who respected and loved animals as much as I did.

I confessed that my one consolation in all this was that the pack was doing much better now. They hadn't mourned like they did when Motaki was killed, they didn't even search for Aipuyi. Instead, they were peaceful and content. The pack was calm for the first time in a long time.

I felt better as we talked, and before we hung up, Jamie expressed a sentiment that touched me deeply.

"Jim, I wish I could've been there for you."

I did, too. Little did I know that soon she would be. 🐾

## CHAPTER 8
# NEW ADVENTURES

## JAMIE

Over the years, Jim had come to Washington, D.C., several times to discuss his projects with his executive producer. He'd always take the opportunity to ask me to lunch or dinner. I'd tell him about the animals I was caring for at the zoo, and he'd tell me about the animals in *his* life—beavers, cougars, and in recent years, the amazing Sawtooth Pack. From across the country I had watched his films and saved his articles that appeared in *National Geographic* magazine.

Between Jim's stories and the photos he had shown me, I felt like I knew the wolves almost as well as he did. I didn't, of course, but I wanted to. I pictured them in their thick winter coats romping through the snow. I could see Kamots, Matsi, and the others greeting Jim with a lick of his face. Kissed by a wolf—what must *that* be like!

Mostly I imagined the howls—those hauntingly soulful sounds that seem to pour out of a wolf as easily as water from a pitcher.

Jim's visits left me exhilarated, but also a bit hollow and sad. As I sat there enthralled with tales of his adventures, I couldn't help but question the life I was living.

My career at the zoo was important to me, and I enjoyed caring for the animals. But I yearned to explore their world. The same dreams that had filled my imagination as a young girl were coming back to me, stronger with each passing year.

For too long, I had pushed my dreams aside.

It was only a few weeks before the airing of his film *Wolf: Return of a Legend* when Jim called to say he'd be in town again and asked me to lunch. By this time, I really wanted to make a change.

During lunch, we talked about our past relationships. In the seven years that we had known each other, this was the first time we really spoke of our personal lives. It was good to finally open up.

Then Jim took a deep breath and told me about his idea for a second film. That's why he was in town.

He was pleased that *Wolf: Return of a Legend* would help dispel some myths, but it seemed to be missing something.

When I asked what he meant, he said, "Well, there were so many problems these past few years that the film seems to go from one catastrophe to another. I didn't fully capture the devotion that these amazing animals have to one another. There's so much more to tell."

"I see what you mean," I replied. "It must be hard to cram three years of experiences into a one-hour film."

He nodded. He felt strongly that Kamots wanted to show him more about the life of wolves. The pack was just coming into its own. Matsi, Amani, and Motomo were almost adults, and he wanted to see them all grow together, especially now that there was harmony in the pack.

He became animated and his eyes sparkled when he said, "And can you imagine how wonderful it would be if pups were born to wolves in the Sawtooth Pack? I'd love to show *that* to the world!"

Jim's enthusiasm was contagious. I thought a sequel was a wonderful idea, and I told him so. I also mentioned that I'd love to meet the wolves someday.

With that, I could see Jim take another deep breath. Then he said that he would need help with the new film, especially recording sound. After a long pause, he looked me straight in the eye and he asked with a smile if I would be interested in coming to Idaho to work with him.

For a split second, I wasn't sure I had heard right. Then it sunk in.

Suddenly I felt like a window that I had been looking through for so long had been flung wide open. Jim and I stared at each other for just a moment. Then I smiled wider than I had in a long time and said yes.

Three weeks later, right before New Year's, I left my safe, comfortable city life behind and boarded a plane for the unknown.

Driving north out of Ketchum, we wound our way up a steep mountain highway. I could see that my first of many new adventures was simply going to be getting to wolf camp.

As we climbed higher and higher, I had to keep swallowing to unplug my ears from the constant change in air pressure. Snow-capped mountains loomed above us on either side. The views were breathtaking, especially at the route's high point, a place called Galena Summit.

Just beyond the summit, the road plunged into the Sawtooth Valley, sharply twisting back and forth down the mountainside. In a matter of minutes, we left behind the steep slopes and entered onto a broad valley floor. Silver-green sagebrush poked above several inches of snow on the ground. Winding its way through the willows was the crystal clear Salmon River.

The changing landscape was so new to me, and so beautiful, I just stared out the window and took it all in.

We continued through the small town of Stanley, where we left the highway and drove west on a dirt road toward the Sawtooth Mountains. I smiled when I recognized their jagged ridges from Jim's films and photographs. I was getting closer to wolf camp ... and my dream.

But first we had to take a hike.

The snow became too deep to continue driving, yet not deep enough for the preferred winter mode of transportation—snowmobiles. So we strapped on our gear and prepared to hoof it the last mile to camp.

I couldn't help but laugh. *This is crazy! Why am I loving it so much?*

Back in Washington about this time I might be pulling up in my driveway with a few bags of groceries, perhaps looking forward to an evening with a good book or a TV show.

Here on the edge of the Sawtooths, as a cold wind whistled down from the mountains, Jim and I were carrying groceries on our backs. I would be spending the night in a tent without electricity or plumbing. I was getting my first taste of what it meant to trade the cozy comforts of a suburban life for the rugged outdoors.

And I couldn't have been happier.

As Meadow Creek came into view, it struck me as the most beautiful place I had ever seen. It immediately felt like home.

Before entering the camp, however, Jim stopped. He tilted back his head, cupped his hands around his mouth, and belted out a long howl. He explained that whenever he was away from camp for a few days, he liked to announce his return in this very special way.

Jim's wolf song drifted off into the distance. For a few seconds all was quiet ...

Then I heard it. A single distant howl rose from somewhere among the trees and floated on the air. Other howls quickly followed.

The pack was responding to Jim's call!

Each howl had a slightly different pitch and was released at a slightly different time. It was like a well-rehearsed choir, with the pack lifting its voice as one, harmonizing in a most beautiful, thrilling way. The sound seemed to come from every direction. It took my breath away.

When we got to camp the first thing I had to do was meet the wolves. So we dropped our bags in the tent and walked over to the enclosure.

The wolves were waiting for us near the gate. They were eager to greet Jim, as always, but also curious about this new person who was with him—me. I suddenly became anxious. Jim was their trusted friend, having known them since they first opened their puppy eyes. But would they trust *me*—a total stranger?

They whined with excitement as we entered the double gate. Once inside, we immediately crouched down so that the powerful animals wouldn't knock us over as they gathered round us.

And gather round they did.

I often compare that first meeting to being engulfed by a fluffy tornado with tongues. That's what it felt like. Their coats had grown out for the winter, so the wolves were especially soft, fluffy, and huge. In my crouched position, they were as tall as I was, and all I could see was gray, white, and black fur swirling around me. Furry bodies enveloped me like warm blankets. Happy wagging tails swished my hair.

Each wolf wanted to be the first to say hello, and I quickly discovered that to a wolf, "hello" means licking every inch of your face. I also learned to keep my mouth closed during such greetings. It was difficult to do because I had a giant urge to smile and laugh at the sheer joy of it all.

So *this* is what it's like to be kissed by a wolf!

I so wanted to wrap my arms around their big furry necks, the way I would hug a large pet dog. But I knew that they weren't pets and shouldn't be treated as such. If they wanted to come to me, I would happily accept their greeting and return it by stroking their muzzle or neck. And if they didn't want to approach me, that was fine, too. In other words, I understood, as Jim did, that everything had to be on their terms.

The enthusiastic greeting continued for several minutes. At some point during the hellos, one of the wolves somehow managed to get his lower tooth stuck up my nose! Of all the scenarios that ran through my mind earlier that day of how this first meeting might go, not one of them included lifting my nostril off a wolf tooth.

Clearly my fear of rejection was unfounded. I think the wolves sensed that I was a friend. I can't say that they completely trusted me on the first day, but they seemed to accept me.

All but one, that is. I looked around and noticed that Lakota was nowhere in sight.

I had expected as much. On our way to camp that morning, Jim had explained that the arrival of anyone new causes great excitement among the wolves. And when the wolves get excited, they tend to pick on the omega, and that lowly position belonged to Lakota. So Lakota would likely keep his distance until things calmed down.

After the friendly greeting, the wolves abruptly turned and trotted away. Their departure was so sudden that for a moment I thought I had offended them. Jim chuckled when he saw the *What did I do?* look on my face.

He assured me all was well. The wolves simply were done meeting me. They had satisfied their curiosity and discovered that I wasn't a threat—two key objectives when encountering any new being. In their world, there was no need to hang around for a polite length of time. It was nothing personal.

I could see that I had a lot to learn about wolves. I knew plenty about them from reading. I knew how to treat them medically and how to care for them. But I had little firsthand experience with how they interacted. That's the priceless knowledge that Jim had been collecting over the last few years. It was knowledge that we both were looking forward to building upon in the years ahead.

With the wolves scattered in the willows and the shy Lakota not yet ready to meet me, I turned my attention to exploring camp.

It was even more impressive than Jim had described.

The large cook tent was particularly comfortable and homey, but the next day it would be coming down. It was too large to heat during the winter, and the roof couldn't handle the heavy snows. So every year about this time, it was dismantled and its contents moved into the smaller, sturdier yurt. That's what we would be doing tomorrow.

On that first night, however, the cook tent was still open for business, and Jim prepared a simple dinner. No gourmet meal ever tasted so delicious.

As we sat by candlelight, we shared more stories from our separate pasts. At one point, we let out a laugh that must have carried loud and clear into the cold, still night because it prompted the wolves to start a howl. We immediately fell silent, closed our eyes, and just listened to the serenade.

After a warm, relaxing evening, it was time for some much needed sleep. I pushed back the flap of the cook tent to head toward the sleep

# LIFE AT
# WOLF CAMP

◄ Glowing from lantern light, our round yurt was the center of activity on winter evenings—from meals and conversation to equipment repair.

◐ During the second half of the wolf project, we moved our camp into the wolves' habitat. Living among the wolves allowed us to observe their behavior in greater detail, and even participate in howls.

◐ We hand-raised the pups for several weeks in the yurt, where the nozzle of the water cooler became an object of endless fascination.

◐ The yurt served as our workshop, where we worked on equipment and planned the scenes for our film.

# SAWTOOTH PACK
# WOLVES

⬆ The Sawtooth Pack, like all wolf packs, was a family.

**AIPUYI**

("One Who Speaks A Lot") was the very vocal sister of Kamots and Lakota.

**AKAI**

("Wise One") was the first wolf in the pack, but we never fully gained his trust.

**AMANI**

("Speaks the Truth") enjoyed playing with all pups, like a favorite uncle.

## CHEMUKH

("Black") became the mate of Kamots and mother of the Sawtooth pups.

## KAMOTS

("Freedom") was the confident and kind alpha male of the pack.

## LAKOTA

("Friend") was the omega—he was the largest but lowest ranking member of the pack.

## MAKUYI

("Wolf") was a sweet and kind female wolf.

## MATSI

("Sweet and Brave") was true to his name, and Lakota's best friend.

## MOTAKI

("Shadow") was a shy and mysterious female.

## MOTOMO

("He Who Goes First") was the most curious about people, watching us for hours at a time.

## WAHOTS

("Likes to Howl") slept next to our tent and serenaded us with his howls.

## WYAKIN

("Spirit Guide") was inseparable from her brother, Wahots.

## SAWTOOTH PUPS

Piyip ("Boy"), Ayet ("Girl"), and Motaki (after the original Motaki) were the Sawtooth pups. Born to Chemukh after mating with Kamots, the pups belonged to the entire pack.

# RUNNING WITH WOLVES TIMELINE

⋀ Throughout the project, we had the privilege of observing four litters of pups. We became trusted friends.

| 1987 | 1988 | 1989 |
|------|------|------|

### 1987

Jim and Jamie meet for the first time.

### 1988

Jim begins the cougar project.

➲ Growing up, we both loved animals. Jim spent time working on a ranch in Wyoming while Jamie was a keeper at the National Zoo. A chance encounter brought us together.

| 1990 | 1991 | 1992 |

**SPRING 1991**

Construction of wolf camp begins

**SUMMER 1991**

Adult wolves Akai and Makuyi join wolf camp. Jim hand-raises the first litter of pups: Kamots, Lakota, Aipuyi, and Motaki. They form the Sawtooth Pack.

**1992**

Makuyi and Akai leave camp.

**SPRING 1992**

Motaki is killed by a cougar.

**SUMMER 1992**

The second litter of pups joins wolf camp: Matsi, Motomo, and Amani.

← Matsi gives Lakota (center) a comforting look, assuring the omega that he won't let the other wolves pick on him too much.

1993

**WINTER 1993**

Jamie joins Jim at wolf camp.

← Filming and photographing curious wolves could sometimes be challenging, but it was always joyful.

⊙ During howls, the omega Lakota (center) tried to remain as unnoticeable as possible, with tail tucked, body lowered, and ears pinned back.

1994

## SPRING 1994

The third litter joins the Sawtooth Pack: Chemukh, Wahots, and Wyakin.

## SUMMER 1994

Jim and Jamie move wolf camp inside the enclosure.

⊱ We always let the wolves approach us; we didn't run after *them*. Everything had to be on their terms.

➔ Companionship, friendship, affection, and more ... By living with wolves and gaining their trust, they revealed to us the relationships that unify a wolf pack.

**1995**          **1996**

**WINTER 1996**

Kamots chooses Chemukh as his mate.

**SPRING 1996**

Chemukh gives birth to Piyip, Ayet, and Motaki.

**SUMMER 1996**

The wolf project comes to an end and the Sawtooth Pack is moved to a permanent home with the Nez Perce tribe of Idaho.

↻ Today, we continue to share our experiences and raise awareness of wolves and the challenges they face.

tent. As I stepped outside, a sharp blast of cold air struck my face. My cheeks became numb. I realized then how remote this place was.

But upon entering the sleep tent, I was greeted by the warmth of a fire that Jim had already lit in the woodstove. Flickering candles on a small homemade desk cast a golden glow on old Navajo blankets that lined the walls. It was all so inviting.

Snuggled beneath flannel sheets and a cozy comforter, my head sunk into soft pillows on the homemade bed. I had never felt more at home.

I awoke to a gorgeous sunny but frosty morning. Jim was already building a fire, and the tent began to warm.

It was going to be a busy day. After a light breakfast of blueberry scones and coffee, we started taking down the large cook tent and moving the kitchen into the yurt.

Everything had its place in this little round tent. Dishes, pots, utensils, dishwashing tubs—they all fit perfectly on shelves or in bins. Baskets and mesh bags hung on the walls for space-saving storage.

With the yurt set up, we turned our attention back to the wolves, specifically Lakota. We hadn't seen him since we arrived in camp, and Jim started to get concerned. I did, too.

Jim told me about a day during the previous spring when he had seen large cougar tracks near the enclosure. While Jim never saw the cougar or any other tracks, he couldn't shake the memory of Motaki's death, and he worried it might happen again. So, we were anxious as we began to search for Lakota.

It was my first chance to explore the wolves' territory. It reminded me of the wondrous times spent exploring the woods behind my house as a young girl, except the woods of my youth didn't include a pack of wolves.

As we searched the forest, ravens cawed from the treetops, announcing our whereabouts. I happened to look over my shoulder and saw the pack following us. Even though I knew there was nothing to fear, it still felt strange being followed by wolves.

The pack walked silently in single file. Kamots took the lead, followed by Matsi, Motomo, and Amani. Motomo's wound from his fight with Aipuyi the previous fall had healed. He had no trace of a limp as I watched him lope gracefully with the others through the snowdrifts. When we stopped, the wolves stopped, too. When we resumed walking, so did they. It almost became a game.

But they didn't make it easy. One kept sneaking up behind me and grabbing the loose leather straps from my snowshoes. And down I went in an embarrassing face-plant into the snow!

After more than an hour of searching, we ended up back where we had started, with no sign of Lakota. The wolves must have figured this little adventure was over, and they trotted off.

As soon as they were out of sight, we heard a rustling behind us in the willows.

Out of the dense bushes crept Lakota!

He had been following us the entire time. He knew that if he showed himself, he'd get our attention. That might make the other wolves jealous, and they'd take out their jealousy on Lakota by picking on him. So, he stayed hidden until the coast was clear.

I was excited to meet this beautiful wolf that Jim had told me so much about. But I was also concerned how Lakota would respond to me, so I knelt down, trying not to intimidate him. I knew that he was incredibly shy and I wondered if he'd continue to keep his distance.

I didn't wonder for long. He slowly and cautiously walked toward me. And when he reached me, he licked my face. It was such a sweet greeting.

Yet, when I ran my hand through his thick winter coat, I felt a twinge of dismay. I could feel the bumps and scabs on his back—spots where the other wolves had nipped at him. This close, I could see that his muzzle was covered with tiny scars where his pack mates had grabbed him in their jaws to show dominance.

Immediately, I felt a special bond with this gentle omega. We sat together for several minutes.

I thought of the little girl who long ago dreamed of befriending a bear. I had grown up believing such things to be merely fantasies. And yet, as Lakota looked at me with his wise amber eyes, I knew that we—two very different creatures—would become lifelong friends.

As time went on, my friendships with all of the wolves blossomed. I was overjoyed that they accepted me into their lives even though I was new to them. I think it helped that I was completely comfortable around animals.

Although we could walk among the wolves, in some ways, there was still too much distance between us. For the new film, Jim wanted to dive deeper into the private lives of the pack. To do that, we had to become so integrated into the pack that they would largely ignore us and go about their daily business of being wolves.

I had a suggestion: Instead of living next to the enclosure, why not move inside it? 🐾

# CHAPTER 9
# TWO LEAPS FORWARD

## JIM

The fence had always been a barrier between the wolves and humans. They could hear us milling about the camp even though trees blocked their view of us. But we knew that unseen conversations, pots banging, and the *thunk* of chopping wood drew the attention of these curious creatures.

So did the clanking and squeaking of the double gates as we opened them and entered the territory. The wolves would come to investigate and greet us. Though we loved the interaction, it took them away from whatever they had been doing, interrupting and changing the very behavior we wanted to observe and film.

Jamie had a hunch that if we moved camp inside the enclosure, the wolves would reveal more of their hidden lives. We would see wolf behaviors that no one ever had.

It made perfect sense.

We didn't move everything. The new camp consisted of only the yurt and a sleep tent for Jamie and me. The downsizing was a way to keep the new camp as simple as possible so as not to disturb the pack.

We decided on a spot at the edge of the big central meadow where the wolves most often played and spent much of their time. We built the yurt on an eight-foot (2.4-m)-high wooden platform, which also included a deck. From there, we had terrific views of the surrounding area.

During construction, the wolves lay in the grass and watched us work ... until they got bored and decided to have a little fun. Not a day went by that these clever canines didn't steal some tool or piece of lumber from where we stored it beneath the deck. Before we lost all our supplies, I figured we'd better fence off our new camp. That had always been the plan, but the wolves' thievery moved up the timetable.

However, before we had a chance to put up the fence, we had a visitor. Jamie and I were setting up the yurt's kitchen area when a large shadowy shape appeared on the canvas wall. It was Kamots. He had climbed the staircase that we thought was too steep for any wolf to attempt. Not Kamots. He was always up for a challenge, and here he was exploring the platform as if he was making sure we were building *our* new home to *his* liking.

By early summer the move was complete. It didn't take long before Jamie's hunch proved correct and we started noticing wolf behavior that was brand new to us.

On the first morning, at daybreak, Jamie and I quietly left our tent and climbed the stairs to the deck. We wanted to see how the pack started their day. What do they do when they first wake up? It seems like a simple thing, but no one had ever witnessed it.

What we saw surprised us.

In the faint light of dawn, we could see that each wolf slept in his own spot on the edge of the forest near our camp. Even though they were at least 15 feet (5 m) apart, they all started stirring at once. It was like they had internal alarm clocks all set to the same time.

Motomo was the first on his feet. He did what I do first thing in the morning—yawn and stretch. He planted his front paws on the ground and pushed back, extending his forelimbs, dropping his chest, and raising his rump. Then he rocked forward and extended his hind limbs. It looked so comfortable, I almost stretched with him.

Next, Motomo walked over to Kamots. The two touched noses as if to say "Good morning." To show proper respect, Motomo tried to keep his head lower than that of the alpha, a difficult task since Kamots was still lying down! Motomo had to nearly rest his head on the ground. A moment later Kamots rose to his feet while Motomo licked the alpha's face and whimpered.

By now, the other wolves had risen and limbered up with a good stretch. Each took his turn greeting Kamots to the new day. Beginning with Matsi, the beta, or second-in-command, and ending with Lakota. After greeting their leader, they turned and greeted one another.

Every morning was the same sweet ritual among the five wolves, the only change being which wolf happened to rise first.

It struck us how important these greetings were. It wasn't politeness and it wasn't habit. It was a reinforcement of the strong bonds among the wolves, that no matter what, they were a family and belonged together.

The pack greeted Jamie and me in much the same way they greeted one another. But we discovered that such greetings could not be forced.

One morning, a crew member wanted to get a shot of the wolves greeting me. I had been out among the pack for a few minutes and we had already said our good mornings, so he asked if I could return to my tent and repeat the process so he could film it.

When I stepped from the tent a second time, the wolves completely ignored me. Their attitude seemed to be, "Oh, it's you. We already said hello to you today."

To the pack, my repeated actions were pointless. It would be like a student entering the classroom, saying good morning to the teacher, and then stepping out in the hall, reentering, and saying good morning again.

We eventually got the shot another morning, but the pack's response was a relief to me. It meant the wolves were reacting less and less to our presence and just being themselves.

We were no longer visitors to the wolf territory, but residents.

A fence may have surrounded our sleep tent, but the motion of its single gate caused no disturbance. It was like passing in and out of a back door in a neighborhood—no one took much notice. Because the wolves saw more of us each day, they paid less attention to us as humans and acted more naturally.

We were also able to observe some of their natural behavior from the high vantage point of the deck. From there, I filmed one of my favorite sequences of wolf play.

It was a warm summer afternoon and the wolves had gathered in the meadow for an especially energetic game of tag. They darted around like a blur of fur, chasing one another as they often did. But this time, when one wolf caught up with a pack mate, he tried as best he could to grab the other's tail. Then, the chasing wolf immediately took off in another direction and became the pursued.

To add an extra element of fun, sometimes a wolf hid behind the dense willows and pounced on an unsuspecting bystander. Then they both took off, one in hot pursuit of the other. It was hilarious!

That same summer brought another surprising observation from the deck.

The meadow was ablaze with colorful wildflowers. I sat and watched the pack slowly pick their way through the tall grass, heads down. It looked like they were smelling the flowers, but I wasn't sure. I grabbed my binoculars and focused in on Motomo. He wasn't sniffing but chewing something—I didn't know what.

I glanced over at Matsi just in time to see him snip a blossom from its stem and chew it. The wolves were eating flowers! Who would have guessed that these meat-eating predators enjoyed a salad now and then?

They were picky salad eaters, too. They weren't just eating any old flower. On closer inspection, it was clear that the wolves were seeking out and eating only shooting stars. These small blossoms consist of a pointy yellow center and bright pinkish purple petals that flare back, making the flower look like a colorful dart.

Jamie—ever the adventurer—tasted the flower and didn't think it had much flavor. But the wolves loved it. Every year they ate this flower and no other. If we hadn't moved camp within the enclosure, we might never have seen this interesting bit of wolf behavior.

For all of its benefits, the move did have one drawback—mice.

Field mice were among the smaller wildlife that inhabited the enclosure. These rodents have it rough. Between the coyotes and foxes lurking on the ground and the owls and hawks patrolling the skies, a mouse spends much of its time trying to avoid being eaten. Add to this list of dangers a pack of wolves and the mice population must've thought nature was playing a cruel joke.

When we moved into the middle of the territory, however, our fenced camp provided a safe zone for the little rodents. Word must have spread that there was now a place to hide out for a while.

Each day brought more unwelcome guests into our humble abode. We really didn't mind, though. We set out nonlethal traps, and releasing the mice back into the meadow simply became one of our daily chores at wolf camp.

Moving camp to be among the wolves was a huge leap forward for the project. Another leap was the addition of our third litter.

# JAMIE

Life among the Sawtooth Pack was all I could've hoped. We were filming and recording intimate behaviors we had never seen or heard before and couldn't dream of getting access to in the wild. Yet, something was missing.

There had been no female in the family for more than six months. We hoped to someday experience the birth of pups and film the adults' reaction to such an event.

Earlier in the spring, as we were making plans for the new camp, Jim made a phone call to his friend Karin, who had provided the pups of what was now the Sawtooth Pack from the shelter she ran in Montana. She told us some exciting news—two mated pairs of her wolves were having litters.

I was giddy with excitement as we drove all day to Montana. When we got to our destination and saw three pups waiting for us, I was overjoyed.

Two of them, a brother and sister, were the typical gray and white hallmark colors of gray wolves. The third was a black female. This beautiful jet-black pup immediately captured our hearts because her parents were the parents of Motaki.

The long trip home gave me a chance to begin the bonding process with these irresistible fuzz balls. They were only 10 days old and needed constant attention. I had given Jim advice about wolf pup care over the years, and now I was thrilled to be able to provide it myself.

As we traveled along, all was quiet as the pups fell asleep flopped on top of one another in a large cardboard box in the back of the van.

Then, after a few hours, one of the pups in the sleeping clump of fur stirred. Soon all three were awake, snarling, wrestling, and bouncing off the cardboard walls.

After about a half hour of this puppy play, we stopped to feed them and clean the messes from their box. Sleep, play, eat became the pattern for the ride back to wolf camp, where the old cook tent, for the third time, became the pups' home for the next several weeks.

Along with the joy of caring for the pups, I had the privilege of naming them.

The Nez Perce (nez PURS) tribe had agreed to provide a permanent home for the wolves on their land after our project was completed. We wanted to honor this agreement by giving the pups Nez Perce names.

I named the gray male Wahots (WA-hotz), Nez Perce for "likes to howl." Did I think he would take more to howling than other wolves? Not a clue. It was just a nice wolf-sounding name. As it turned out, he was one of the best howlers in the pack.

Wahots's sister I called Wyakin (WHY-ah-kin), or "spirit guide." In Nez Perce traditions, a *wyakin* reveals itself to children as they seek to become adults. Their wyakin protects them and helps them deal with life's conflicts and questions. It's a beautiful and powerful tradition and seemed an appropriate name for a beautiful and powerful animal.

At first, I called the black female Chemukh-Chemukh Ayet. It was a mouthful, but it came from the Nez Perce words for "black" (*chemukh-chemukh*) and "lassie" or "girl" (*ayet*), so "Black Lassie." The name wasn't very imaginative, but it had a nice ring to it, and soon her name simply became Chemukh (cha-MUK).

Those first few weeks of raising the playful pups were precious times that I wouldn't trade for anything. Occasionally, their play got out of hand and we had to instill a little discipline.

During one incident, Wyakin sunk her sharp tiny teeth into a rag I was using to clean her. The rag was small and she could have swallowed it, so I needed to wrest it from her. She hung on as if she were bringing down a moose! When I pulled, she let out such a nasty snarl that I had to go into "mother wolf" mode. I flipped her on her back and growled. She got the message and let go of her prize.

Wyakin was the feistiest of the litter. Her brother, Wahots, was more observant and clever. He would often take a moment to watch and size up a situation before jumping into the action. For instance, if his sister was trying to grab an old leather work glove from Chemukh, Wahots would wait for the two to exhaust themselves and take the opportunity to steal the glove.

Despite their differences, the brother and sister were inseparable. They enjoyed wrestling and laying their forelimbs on each other's back, one trying to dominate the other.

Chemukh was much more timid. If she won a tug-of-war, it was only because her opponent was distracted by some other object, or by food.

It's not that she was weaker than her littermates. She wasn't. It was about personality. Chemukh lacked tenacity, the ability to grab hold of something and not let go, literally and figuratively. I wondered if she might one day become the pack's female omega.

After a few weeks, it was time to introduce meat into the pups' diet. In the wild, this happens by an adult wolf regurgitating—throwing up—food, which the pups then eat.

In a kitchen tent, this happens by cutting up raw chicken into small pieces, mixing it with milky formula, and heating the disgusting concoction until it's as warm as it would be coming from an adult wolf's stomach. It smelled as bad as it sounds—to us. But the pups gobbled it up!

Soon the pups' teeth grew enough to start them on solid food. We fed them larger chicken parts instead of cutting up the chicken into pieces. I was shocked at how ferociously these cute little animals tore into the meat.

At one feeding, Wyakin swallowed an entire chicken thigh almost as big as her head. I could see the shape of the meat and bone protruding from her throat. She gagged and jerked in an effort to get it down. It looked like she was going to choke to death. Either that or the chicken piece was going to burst through her skin!

Before I could decide how to help her, she managed to finally down the food and dove in for more. I just shook my head in disbelief ... or maybe in awe.

This sort of behavior is natural for a wolf. In the wild, when a pack succeeds in making a kill, they eat as much as possible, because there's no guarantee when their next successful hunt will be.

However, even Wyakin, the biggest eater of the bunch, couldn't always finish a meal. So, she would stockpile some food for later. She usually chose to hide leftover meat in the wooden "den" that we had built for the pups. It was sort of like a doghouse. Wyakin thought she was being sneaky and clever by stashing the meat under an old blanket in the den. But she couldn't out-clever her brother.

Wahots, always watchful, was onto her.

He hid behind the den, and when his sister came out, he'd sneak in and eat the hidden cache.

When Wyakin went to retrieve her leftovers, she was in for a rude surprise. The confused look on her little face was priceless! She pawed at the blanket and poked her head beneath it. I could picture the thought bubble, "Seriously, this is ridiculous! I know I put it here somewhere." Then she wandered around the pen looking under leaves, sticks, and other blankets, perhaps thinking she had merely forgotten where she hid the meat.

This little escapade happened over and over and over. And poor little Wyakin never caught on.

Based on the pups' appetites, I thought nothing could upset their stomachs. But I couldn't have been more wrong.

At the beginning of June, the pups were five weeks old and not yet old enough to be left alone, so we started taking them overnight when we went to town for supplies. A small pen made of wire mesh fit nicely in the back of the van for these journeys. I was excited as we gathered the pups for their first trip.

My excitement was short-lived.

As soon as we started to drive, Wahots began to throw up. A moment later Chemukh and Wyakin joined in. It was like a vomit relay race—when one finished, the other started. These weren't gentle spit-ups, either; they were stinky, messy explosions!

After at least two rounds of tossing up their breakfast of raw chicken and formula, the pups were doing just fine.

I, on the other hand, was ready to pass out.

Jim tried his best to keep the van steady on the twisty mountain road, but the nauseating pool of vomit still sloshed back and forth in the pen. Some of it spilled through the wire mesh and onto the plastic tarp that I had laid over the entire back floor.

I bent over the walls of the pen to soak up as much of the slop as I could with handfuls of newspaper. The stink was overwhelming. To make matters worse, I had to fend off vomit-soaked Wahots and Wyakin, who were having a ball grabbing the newspaper and tearing it to shreds.

By the time we reached Ketchum, the pups were full of energy and ready to play. I was exhausted and in dire need of fresh air.

After buying groceries, charging camera batteries, and shipping off film for processing, we repeated the vomit voyage up into the mountains.

I thought after two spew-filled drives the pups might be exhausted when we finally arrived at wolf camp. But the barf fest was forgotten the moment they saw the adult wolves. I don't know who whined with more excitement—the puppies or the adults. The adults clamored over one another to get the best position to greet the pups through the chain-link fencing. It was every bit as sweet as Jim had described it in years past.

Throughout June, we made four trips back and forth to Ketchum to ship film and pick up supplies for the new camp. We took the pups with us each time so that we could continue to bond with them. Part of *my* bonding process was cleaning up their vomit.

We tried withholding food from them the morning of the trip or even the night before. It didn't matter. They still hurled as soon as we hit the road. But I had learned my lesson—I always traveled with rags and buckets.

As other litters had done before, the pups graduated from the pen in the tent to the puppy enclosure outside. Then, finally, on a warm, clear morning in August, at the age of 12 weeks, the pups were ready to join the pack. This time we would release them from our new camp in the middle of the wolves' territory.

The adult wolves had been lured into the lock-off. That cleared the way for Jim and me to bring the pups from the puppy enclosure to inside our little fenced camp without getting mobbed.

"It's a big day," Jim said to Wyakin as he carried her from the puppy enclosure to our tents. He set her down inside the fencing that surrounded our sleep tent and elevated yurt to join Wahots and Chemukh, who were already tearing around our camp stealing anything that wasn't nailed down.

Jim and I both knew that this litter was a very special one. Either Wyakin or Chemukh could eventually become the wolf that gives birth to a litter, right here at wolf camp. That was a day we dreamed about.

But first things first. It was time for the meet and greet.

Jim signaled by walkie-talkie to release the adults. They busted out of the lock-off like thoroughbreds breaking out of the gate at a horse race.

"Here they come," I said with anticipation. The wolves splashed across the creek and raced through the meadow to greet the newest pack members.

As the adults ran up to the fence, Wahots and Wyakin eagerly ran up to greet them through the chain-link. Timid Chemukh, however, stayed back, hiding behind our sleep tent.

We kept the pups in our fenced camp area most of the day so that everyone could get used to one another. The adults passed the time by bringing the pups gifts of bones and deer hide. It was so endearing the way they pushed the presents through the fence with their paws or nose.

The hours ticked by. The sun peaked and started its slow descent toward the west. Then in the afternoon, I placed my hand on the latch, took a deep breath, and said, "Okay, this is it. Meet your new family." I opened the gate and stood by with my sound gear to record what would happen.

It wasn't what I expected.

I thought the pups would charge out of the gate. Instead, they stayed where they were, looking a bit sheepish and uncertain. Kamots sensed their apprehension. He walked over and bestowed gentle licks on all of them. It was yet another duty performed with grace and kindness by the good alpha.

The reassurance from Kamots gave Wyakin enough courage to step out. Wahots followed. They both bypassed Kamots and went straight to Matsi, who seemed to be calling them over with a whining melody. I was captivated by their conversation. I only wish I understood what they were saying.

The young brother and sister greeted each adult wolf and then dutifully flipped over on their backs. I could see that their integration into the pack was off to a smooth start, even though Wahots was having a little trouble keeping up with all the confusion and excitement.

Chemukh seemed much more unsure.

She avoided the adults altogether and trotted off to hide in the willows. That wasn't a good sign. Although she came out of hiding an hour later to play with Wyakin, she seemed too afraid to approach the adults. When they trotted toward her, she ran away.

Clearly this youngster didn't know the rules of a wolf pack and needed to be educated. When the adults caught up with the fleeing Chemukh, she quickly rolled over, not out of respect for the social order but in fear. Her move didn't stop the adults from snarling to voice their displeasure. It was a rocky start for the timid female.

The pups and adults continued to get acquainted, but apparently the excitement was a bit much for one of the newcomers.

I was putting away my sound gear in the tent when I heard a faint whining. I assumed it was coming from the other side of the fence. But then I got the uneasy feeling that I was being watched. I turned and there was little Wahots poking his head out from under the cot.

He must have stepped back through the gate unnoticed. He looked at me with a bewildered expression as if to say, "Where did everyone go? Where's my sister? What am I supposed to do now?"

My heart went out to him. I knew he was glad to be with his new pack mates, but I think he also found them a bit scary. Matsi understood. He was waiting for Wahots as I led the pup back through the gate. Matsi's presence reassured him that everything was all right, and the two trotted off together.

After a day of excitement and anxiety, Jim and I finally had a chance to just relax on the deck. The rays of the setting sun bathed the Sawtooths in a fiery yellow-orange glow unlike any sunset I had ever seen.

Before I joined Jim in Idaho, he had often spoken of how the light of the rising and setting sun played on the massive granite peaks. As he talked, I'd close my eyes and imagine the scene that he painted with his words. I loved it. Still, I sometimes thought he was exaggerating, perhaps to entice me to visit.

He wasn't exaggerating. The views were spectacular, and never so much as on this peaceful evening.

To the west, the shadows of the trees stretched across the meadow. Here and there slices of light momentarily blinded our view of the wolves as the sun played peekaboo between tall pines. Shielding our eyes, we could see the adults giving the pups a tour of their new home. Wahots and Wyakin stuck close to Matsi. Chemukh trailed behind, even farther back than Lakota, but it was clear the pack had accepted her. That was a great relief.

We now had a full wolf pack—an extended family of young and adult, male and female, brothers, sisters, cousins, and uncles, both blood and adopted.

In so many ways, the relationships in the pack mirrored those in human families. We already knew that Kamots was the head of his family. He would instill discipline and maintain order.

Matsi seemed to be well on his way to becoming the puppy sitter of the pack. We would find out soon enough just how seriously he took his job.

What about a favorite uncle? I had one of those as I was growing up. So did Jim. Who would take on this role for the pups, and what would that look like?

Would Wyakin and Wahots continue to be inseparable, as they had been since birth?

Most of all we wondered about the relationship between Chemukh and Wyakin. Females in a pack can be bitter rivals as they compete for the right to breed with the alpha. At the moment, Wyakin seemed to have the inside track in that competition. Would the future be different?

The evening slipped into a star-filled night as we quietly mulled over these questions. There was no rush. The wolves would reveal the answers in due time, of that we were certain. 🐾

## CHAPTER 10
# FRIENDS
# FOR LAKOTA

## JIM

The moment Jamie agreed to come to Idaho, I knew that the best days of the wolf project—and the best days of my life—were ahead. Every moment was brighter, happier, and filled with greater promise because we were together. My friends and family could see it. The wolves sensed it, too. They took to her immediately and she to them.

She understood them.

I guess part of that rare quality came from her years of caring for animals at the zoo. Part may even have come from my stories of the pack, those phone calls or letters to her over the years. But most of it was Jamie herself. She simply had the ability to understand what these wild creatures were thinking and feeling. I won't go so far as to say she could talk to them, but she sure could listen.

She was especially close to Lakota, who always seemed to need a friend. I often photographed their visits. I remember one in particular that has stayed with me.

It was the middle of winter, not long after Jamie first joined me at camp. She knelt on the ground among the willows. Lakota circled her, came around from the side, and placed his paw on her shoulder. Jamie spoke a few soothing words and gently stroked his face and thick winter fur. Mostly, they just sat there, enjoying each other's company.

I was moved by the tenderness she showed Lakota, tenderness he so desperately needed. He trusted her, and trust is not something a wolf gives out readily. It's reserved for a treasured few.

# JAMIE

If Kamots was the Sawtooth Pack's head, Lakota was its heart.

Lakota, the omega wolf, was the lowest ranking member of the pack. He had taken over this position from Motaki after her death. By "taken over," I don't mean he volunteered for it. He did not. The other wolves simply showed through their more dominant behavior that they would not accept the omega role. Lakota reluctantly accepted it.

Lakota possessed the qualities that made him suited to be an omega. He was shy and gentle and the least aggressive member of the pack.

He also was the most playful, and knew how to get his pack mates to play. We often watched Lakota approach Kamots in a play bow to entice a game of tag. Or if a piece of deer hide was lying around, Lakota might toss it in the air in front of Matsi, coaxing him to grab an end and have a tug-of-war.

Such play is important because it keeps the mood of the pack light and friendly. That makes life better for every wolf, but especially for the omega, because in addition to being the instigator of play, the omega is the pack scapegoat. So the happier the wolves are, the less reason they have to blame the omega for anything.

The worst times for Lakota often occurred during pack rallies.

The stereotype of a lone wolf howling at night during a full moon is a myth. Wolves howl day or night and whether the moon is out or not.

It usually started with one wolf, head thrown back and eyes shut, letting out a soulful *Aaaoooooooooo*. The others would quickly join in and gather around Kamots, keeping their head lower than his. The powerful surge of sound could be heard far across the landscape.

As the intensity of the howling increased, we could see the wolves getting worked up. They would get fidgety, and the howling seemed to become something of a competition in what are called pack rallies. That often led to displays of dominance. Amani might snarl at Motomo. Matsi might pin Amani. Kamots might growl at Motomo.

Most of the aggression, however, was turned toward Lakota.

Lakota knew he might suffer abuse during a rally, but his deep desire to howl was strong. He usually stood off to the side, perhaps to make himself less visible. As the rest of the pack lifted their voices, we could see Lakota trying to join in.

I could practically feel his voice bubbling up inside him, and I found myself lifting my head and jutting out my chin in anticipation. Finally, he let go. He burst forth with a howl that soared into the air and melded with the rest of the chorus.

It was so beautiful ... and all too brief.

Before long, the wolves would get more and more worked up as the rally reached a point of frenzy. Then Amani or Motomo would dash at Lakota, pinning him down and nipping at his fur.

It was agonizing to witness. Yet, we had to resist interfering. A distinct social hierarchy is crucial to a healthy pack.

Lakota wasn't an outcast. The omega is cherished within the pack as much as the alpha, and is just as important. Without a scapegoat, tensions could rise uncontrollably. It was harsh and unfair treatment, yet completely necessary to keep peace and harmony in the pack. Every wolf, including Lakota, understood this in ways that we never will. He accepted his role without complaint.

Lakota's omega role was evident in everything he did, even the way he stood. He tucked his tail, drooped his shoulders, and lowered his head, all in an attempt to make himself appear smaller and to show submission to the other wolves.

So I was blown away one day when I realized that Lakota was actually the biggest wolf in the pack! When it came to determining roles in the pack's hierarchy, personality was clearly a lot more important than size or strength.

No name was more fitting than that of Lakota ("friend"). He was a friend to every wolf in the pack, and they cared about him. True, it wasn't always evident, at least not to human eyes. But one wolf clearly did show Lakota his care and friendship every day. That wolf was Matsi.

Matsi was the pack's beta wolf, a sort of second-in-command. He had a considerable amount of authority within the pack, and he often used it to protect Lakota. This was especially true at feedings.

During one meal in particular, Jim filmed Kamots and Matsi feasting on a carcass. Matsi was allowed to eat at the same time as the alpha. They usually ate on opposite sides. The different "seats around the table" meant Jim could always find a good angle from which to film the sights and sounds of mealtime.

As a wolf digs into a carcass, the nose pulls up and the lips curl back so that the teeth can tear into the flesh. The wolf's paws brace against the carcass while its powerful jaws rip away the meat. Sounds of smacking rise through the air. Crunching, too. Jaws and teeth chomp through bones as easily as a human munches celery sticks.

Blotches of pink and red stain the wolf's face. Tufts of the prey's fur stick to the wolf's muzzle until the wolf shakes or sneezes them off.

It's not exactly a portrait of good manners, by human standards.

With all the tugging and tearing, scraps of meat tend to be flung in all directions. During this particular feeding, Lakota tried to pick up one of these morsels, but he dropped it when Matsi growled and chased him away. The pecking order must be maintained, and Lakota would have to wait his turn.

As Matsi returned to his meal, Amani, who also was waiting to eat, figured he'd give Lakota a double dose of discipline. He growled at the omega, tackled him, flipped him over, and straddled him. Lakota looked like he was trapped in a cage formed by Amani's four long legs.

Seeing the ruckus, Matsi charged into Amani and knocked him off Lakota. We could hardly believe it. Matsi was showing Amani that he had gone too far. Matsi had disciplined Lakota for eating out of order, but when Amani piled on, the beta wolf came to the rescue.

And it wasn't the only time.

Once during a pack rally, the wolves formed a mob around Lakota. They snarled at him, heaped on top of him, and nipped at his fur. He tried to crawl out from under the fray but he was pinned down.

Then suddenly, like a superhero, Matsi burst into the scene. He didn't knock anyone off the pile this time. Instead, he did something even braver. He wedged himself between Lakota and his tormentors. By doing so, he gave Lakota a chance to crawl out and escape.

Matsi hadn't always been so kind. As a yearling, the future beta did his part in forcing Lakota into the omega position. But after roles were established, Matsi became extremely gentle. He kept order but never joined the others in picking on the omega. Rather, he stood by to make sure Lakota was okay. If he saw things get out of hand, he charged in.

Matsi gave Lakota much more than protection. He gave him freedom.

The two wolves often spent time together away from the rest of the pack. At these times, Lakota could set aside his omega role and be free of its burdens. He could just be a wolf.

One of the happiest sights of the entire project was Matsi and Lakota playing in a snowy field. Lakota held his head high and wagged his tail with delight. He jumped on Matsi's back to play—something he would never do in the presence of the others.

Matsi didn't mind a bit. He dropped to the ground and they both rolled in the snow. Then they stood on their hind legs and pushed against each other with their forelimbs in a mock fight, like a couple of sparring stallions ... or perhaps they were dancing.

Finally, they chased each other through the field and around the trees before resting side by side.

I never saw two wolves that genuinely enjoyed each other's company so much. They were best friends.

We were grateful to Matsi for showing us how much wolves care for one another. But what we witnessed was more than just caring. Matsi showed a quality that Kamots had shown Jim—a quality that is usually attributed only to humans.

Matsi showed compassion.

Who would have guessed that such tenderness was part of the hidden daily lives of wolves? What more would the Sawtooth Pack reveal to us? We could hardly wait to find out. 🐾

## CHAPTER 11

# CALL
## OF THE WOLF

# JAMIE

To me, nothing is more mysterious about wolves than their howls. From the moment I first heard the chorus of the Sawtooth Pack, I became obsessed with capturing these and all of the other wondrous sounds of a wolf pack.

I learned how to operate the recording and mixing equipment and threw myself into the world of sound with a passion. While Jim carried his cameras and tripod around the enclosure, I carried my 12-foot (4-m) telescoping boom-pole, microphone, headphones, and recording pack.

When a wolf was howling, I got as close as I could without disturbing the singing. I extended the boom to position the microphone in the direction of the wolf's upturned face. The tone was loud and clear.

I didn't always want to record so close. I needed some faraway and mid-range sounds to give the audience of our new film the full range of experiences of living with wolves in the wilderness. So, I recorded sound at different distances from the wolves.

Sometimes, however, I wanted my microphone as close to the action as possible. I'm talking about mealtime.

To watch a pack of wolves eat from a distance doesn't show what's really happening. The viewer can't get a sense of the voracious appetite, the single-minded purpose with which these carnivores tear into a carcass.

But to view and listen to this event close-up is to experience nature at its most raw.

The sights and sounds of the feeding are at once terrible and beautiful. The juicy smacking of tongue and teeth against flesh and the crunching of bones are among the sounds of a wolf's nature, and I did all I could to record them.

The wolves, of course, knew full well that we were there, but we had gained their trust. Now and then I'd hold the microphone too close and a wolf would grab for it or take a whack at it. I'd pull up a little but stay as long as the wolves would let me.

I recorded other nature sounds, too—singing birds, babbling brooks, rustling leaves, whistling winds, the bugle call of an elk, and the absolute silence of night, to name just a few. But the wolves' howls are what thrilled me the most.

After listening so intently through my headphones for many, many hours, I found that I could identify each wolf by his or her howl or other vocalizations, even when I couldn't see them.

Lakota's voice was the most beautiful. When I first heard it one winter's night, I could scarcely believe the rich tones that were coming through my headphones. His mournful song rose through the cold evening air and sailed across the sky.

It struck me that Lakota was singing the blues. He seemed to be crying out with an anthem for the omega, for all the omegas of the world. Tears flowed from my eyes as the long, sad howl hung in the air until the last note finally faded into the darkness.

While the song of Lakota could make me well up with emotion, the song of Wahots could make us laugh. It also could scare the daylights out of us.

Wahots couldn't carry a tune as well as Lakota, but he sure could belt it out. He slept right up against the fence by our tent, literally an arm's length from my head. We could hear his rhythmic breathing, which lulled us into a deep sleep ...

Then when he let loose a howl during the night, our eyes popped wide open and we nearly fell out of bed. It was like a siren going off in the tent.

Wahots howled with an exuberant energy, but he didn't know when to quit.

As the alpha, Kamots usually started a howl, followed quickly by the rest of the pack. The song would get louder and louder and more robust until it reached its glorious peak. Then the wolves would stop nearly at the same instant, letting the last soulful sounds drift away and echo off the mountains.

All but Wahots.

He often wanted to roll right into another verse. So he'd take another deep breath, rear back his head, and begin, *Aooo.* That's as far as he'd get before realizing no one else was singing along. Then he'd stop abruptly, perhaps embarrassed, like a child at a school concert starting a song at the wrong time.

We joked that his *Aooo* was more like an *A-oops*. Wahots never did get the hang of it, but he still loved to howl, and we loved to listen.

I took every opportunity to record as many wolf sounds as possible. I wanted to capture not only their howls, but their barks, yips, and yelps. Their sneers, snarls, and growls. Their sighs, whimpers, and whines.

It took a lot of patience, but I was able to compile an extensive library of wolf vocalizations.

My favorite times to record were during winter evenings and nights. Just as the cold, dry air was clean and crisp, so too were the sounds that traveled through it. In the still of night, I could hear a falling pine cone tumble through the boughs of a tree across the meadow.

That was the quality I wanted for the sound track of the film, so I did much of my recording during the cold winter nights.

That's also when the wolves did much of their howling. They rarely slept through the night. Instead they woke up every two or three hours, occasionally to howl. Sometimes they howled in response to some other sound—a hooting owl, a barking coyote in the distant forest, or a rustling of leaves.

Sometimes the wolves seemed to be howling just to check up on one another:

"Are you there?"

"I'm here."

"Are you okay?"

"Yes. You?"

"I'm fine. Good night."

"Good night."

Recording sound wasn't easy during winter nights. In fact, *nothing* was easy during winter nights.

Wolf camp was located in one of the coldest places in the United States. Temperatures often dipped below minus 10°F (–23°C) and sometimes as low as minus 40°F (–40°C).

The wolves seemed completely oblivious to the harsh weather. Their double layer of fur thickened as the season approached and held in their body heat much better than multiple layers of clothing held in ours. Even during the windiest, most bitter-cold nights, they didn't seek shelter beneath a fallen tree or in the dense willows. Rather, they lay out in the open meadow in their usual sleep spots, completely exposed to winter's fury.

We humans, on the other hand, were all too happy to have the shelter of our tent and the warmth from our woodstove. But when the fire went out during the bitter night, everything froze. I often kept a bottle of water in bed with me so that my body heat would keep it from becoming a block of ice.

I kept my sound gear in bed with me, too. Each night before turning in, I set up an outside microphone wired to the tape deck beneath the blankets. When the wolves woke me with their howling, all I had to do was push the record button, slip on my headphones, lie back, and listen.

Lying in bed, my eyes closed, I could picture who was howling and where. I had become that familiar with each wolf's song and I knew where each wolf slept. Every time I witnessed such a serenade, I felt privileged to experience one of nature's most mysterious and beautiful events.

Wolves probably howl for more reasons than we can fathom, and with subtle differences that have meanings known only to them. Yet we're certain that one of the main purposes of howling is to reaffirm the unity of the pack, to solidify the bonds of the family. We were constantly surprised by just how strong those bonds are. 🐾

## CHAPTER 12

# FAMILY TIES

## JIM

As the project rolled into its fourth year, I was happier than I remembered ever being. Jamie and I were witnessing daily the secrets and surprises of the Sawtooth wolves. More importantly, we were witnessing them together.

That spring, I took Jamie to a place that held special meaning for us. It was the pond, not far from Ketchum, where I had filmed a family of beavers seven years earlier. My trip to Africa had been prompted by the need to take a break from editing the film. And my stopover in Washington, D.C., was for the purpose of meeting with my executive producer.

Thus, because of that film and the woodland creatures that inspired it, Jamie and I found each other. It seemed only fitting that there, amid the shimmering pond waters, lively brook trout, and high snow-capped mountains, I asked Jamie to marry me.

Back at wolf camp, watched over by one of our trusted caretakers, the Sawtooth family waited for us.

Families. We were discovering with every passing day that *that's* what wolf packs are all about.

As we watched young Wahots, Wyakin, and Chemukh grow and assimilate into the pack, we were struck yet again by how similar human and wolf families really are, especially in their personal relationships.

For instance, once we moved into the enclosure, we witnessed how wolves, like humans, welcome one another to the new day. Unlike humans, though, the wolves never held back their affection.

The previous night may have included bickering and snarling, as the pack finished off the remains of a deer carcass, yet the next morning, they all greeted one another warmly.

It wasn't that they forgave each other; there simply was nothing to forgive. Conflicts were part of the pack's social behavior and helped maintain order. The bonds between the wolves were too strong to let these arguments interfere with the unity of the pack. They didn't hold grudges.

Living in the wolves' territory, we noticed signs of pack unity and devotion throughout the day. If two wolves passed each other, they almost always rubbed shoulders or exchanged quick licks, like two friends exchanging a nod, hug, or handshake when passing on the street.

Family affection was shown in other ways, too.

Pairs of wolves often lie next to each other to relax. Wahots and Wyakin went one step further—they lay on top of each other.

Usually Wyakin rested her head on Wahots's neck, a pattern of behavior we had seen even when they were mere weeks old. It was a show of dominance by the feisty sister, but one that was mixed with affection and playfulness.

After a while, she would nip at her brother's ear, which signaled a friendly game of jaw wrestling. Their necks twisted and turned as they tried to clamp down on each other's snout—all from a reclined position. It was fun to watch this good-natured play between brother and sister.

Playfulness is one part of wolf behavior that people find most surprising.

Before the project began, I had expected the pups to romp around and to latch on to all sorts of objects. But I thought adult wolves would be nothing but serious. After all, surviving in the wilderness is serious business. And yet, play was a major part of their day no matter what age.

Besides the usual games of tail tag and tug-of-war, the wolves loved to play with almost anything that wasn't bolted or rooted down. Everything became a toy. This included inedible parts of a carcass, such as an antler or a piece of hide.

They were especially curious about any object we had touched, like an article of clothing or a piece of filming equipment. If we laid hands on it, the wolves wanted it. We quickly learned to never put anything down—it would be swiped in seconds. Still, walking into the enclosure could be like walking through a crowd of pickpockets.

One winter day, I was filming the wolves' delightful reaction to a snowfall. I had draped a raincoat over the camera to keep it dry. With my eye pressed against the eyepiece, I didn't realize Kamots was sneaking up on me.

First, I felt a gentle tug. Then ... *WHOOSH!* The coat was gone.

I looked up to see Kamots bounding through the snow with a formerly very nice raincoat. It was shredded in minutes.

Kamots's bold personality made him the pack's number one thief. He was usually the first to steal anything left unguarded, whether it was a glove, a lens cap, or a notebook. Once Kamots or any other wolf had something in his or her jaws, it was nearly impossible to get it back.

The only chance was to distract the culprit with another object.

So, I always carried an old ragged piece of cloth with me to use as trade. It usually worked, especially with Kamots because he was so curious. If he had stolen something of value, I waved the rag to get his attention and then I placed it on the ground.

He would stand still for a moment and look at the rag, almost like he was weighing his options, wondering if this new thing was of greater value than the object clenched between his teeth. He already knew something about what he possessed. But the rag was brand new to him.

Typically, he dropped what he held and trotted over to the rag, while I quickly retrieved what he had dropped.

Of all the objects in camp, the one that interested Kamots the most was my hat. It was an old, tattered, wide-brimmed Australian bush hat and Kamots wanted it badly.

Whenever I was concentrating on filming or working on a piece of equipment, Kamots would slowly come up behind me. I rarely heard his silent steps, but I knew he was there. I knew his game. Just as he was about to grab the brim of the hat, I pulled away. He was always a split second too late.

One day I decided to let Kamots win.

I saw him watching me out of the corner of my eye as I pretended to fiddle with my camera. He approached stealthily from behind as usual. I could sense him getting closer ... and closer ... until I felt his warm breath on the back of my neck.

The next thing I felt was a sharp tug and the hat was off!

Kamots couldn't have been more pleased with himself. After dozens of tries, he finally had his prize. He danced around the meadow, flipping the hat into the air and catching it in his mouth. Matsi watched jealously.

At one point the hat landed over Kamots's face. He darted around the meadow blindly. It was like watching a cartoon. Then he plowed through the thick willows, still with the hat covering his eyes, and with Matsi hot on his heels.

That was the last I saw of my hat.

# JAMIE

Winter brought a certain peculiar pastime. When the ponds and creeks froze, bubbles formed within the ice. The wolves were fascinated by these bubbles, and we were fascinated by how the wolves tried to reach them.

They scratched at the ice, pressed on it, and slammed their forepaws down on it. It was remarkable to watch them recognize a problem and try to figure out a way to solve it.

Though they were never able to reach the bubbles through the thick ice, there was something else that the wolves did figure out. And how they did it mystifies us to this day.

It was midwinter. We had placed a light in a tree near the yurt for night filming. We ran a heavy-duty orange electrical cord along a sturdy limb, connecting the lights to a generator on the deck. We used a ladder to reach the limb, which was at least a dozen feet (4 m) off the ground.

The wolves sat in the snow and watched us work with great interest.

After filming that evening, we unplugged the cord and went to bed. We would take down the cord in the morning.

But when we awoke, the cord had already been taken down ... sort of.

The snow was littered with pieces of orange insulation and exposed wire. The cord had been shredded to bits! Jim and I stood on the deck with our mouths open. We couldn't believe it. We kept turning our heads from the limb to the bright orange mess before us and blurted out the simple one-word questions that raced through our minds.

"What?"

"How?"

Obviously, the pack had somehow gotten hold of the cord during the night. But the wolves couldn't jump up to the limb. No way.

We ran through other possibilities. What about a raccoon or a squirrel? Nope, not with the wolves right there. Wahots especially would have been alerted if prey came sneaking by because he always slept right next to the fence near our tent.

If the wolves had somehow gotten onto the deck, they might have been able to jump from the railing up to the limb. Or they could have pulled on the plug to bring down the cord.

The only problem with this scenario is that a tall fence completely surrounded our mini-camp, including the staircase to the deck. If they tried to climb the fence, which was nearly impossible, we would have heard the racket.

Jokingly I said, "Maybe they made a wolf pyramid."

I pantomimed three wolves on the bottom, two standing on top of them, and one to form the peak. Another wolf would then get a running start, bound up the pyramid, and take a flying leap off of the top wolf to grasp the cord.

We laughed at the thought of it, especially how the pack probably would have tumbled in a heap from the force of the jumping wolf.

Despite our racing imaginations, the wolves never showed us how they pulled off this trick of all tricks. It's a mystery to this day.

When we think back on that incident, we picture the wolves watching us string up the cord. Were they already hatching a plan? We would never underestimate the intelligence of these animals, nor their ability to cooperate. They showed us both qualities over and over again.

Cooperation was precisely what the Sawtooth Pack demonstrated one cold day in November when some of the wolves concocted a plan to outwit their fearless leader.

We had just brought the wolves a young road-killed deer. The pack had eaten only a few days before, so no one would starve if they couldn't get a piece of this small meal. Even so, wolves eat whenever they can, and everyone was hoping for at least a snack.

Kamots and a few other wolves had devoured nearly the entire deer. All that remained were two disembodied hind legs, a small part of the torso, and a few scraps lying next to the carcass. Kamots had his still-hungry eyes on all of these tasty morsels. Amani and Motomo faced Kamots with whimpering pleas, but all they received for their whining was a growl. It looked like there would be no snack for them this time.

Or would there?

Amani and Motomo continued to whine. We thought they were communicating with Kamots, but based on what happened next, it seemed they were communicating with each other.

All of a sudden Motomo made a mad dash, grabbed one of the scraps, and ran. Kamots took the bait and chased after Motomo.

With the deer unguarded, Amani quickly moved in and snatched one of the hind legs. Kamots realized his mistake and turned just in time to see Amani take off for the dense thicket of willows with the deer leg in his mouth. Kamots followed at a sprint. Motomo then dropped his scrap, ran back for the other hind leg, and took off in the opposite direction.

Kamots stopped and turned his head from side to side as he watched both wolves flee with their prizes. Meanwhile Lakota, who hadn't stood a chance to share in this meal, was downing the morsel that Motomo had dropped.

We had to stop ourselves from laughing out loud at the ingenious way these two mid-ranking wolves had outsmarted their leader.

Kamots took it all in stride. He didn't pick a fight with them afterward, and they didn't rub it in. There was no lingering sign that anything out of the ordinary had occurred. Instead, I imagined Kamots thinking to himself the wolf equivalent of "Well played, mates, well played."

Amani and Motomo weren't the only food thieves.

Shortly after joining the pack, Wyakin returned to her old tricks of hiding food. During a meal, she sometimes would leave the carcass to carry pieces of meat into the thick willows. As always, she thought she was being clever and sneaky. But Wahots knew exactly what his sister was up to.

When Wyakin trotted off with some scraps, Wahots looked up from his meal to watch where she was going. I could imagine what was going through his head as Wyakin casually came back to the carcass: "Okay, so that's the willow where you're hiding it this time. Got it."

Later that afternoon, when all the wolves were sleeping off their big meal, Wahots stepped away, trotted over to the willow, and returned several minutes later licking his chops.

Wyakin spent the next hour probing the willows and peeking under logs, looking completely befuddled. She never caught on, just like when they were pups. As intelligent as wolves are, some are definitely smarter than others.

Affection ... playfulness ... cooperation ... friendly sibling rivalries ... Each relationship within the Sawtooth family brought out the different personality traits of the wolves.

The friendship between Matsi and Lakota, for instance, showed Matsi's protective nature. The pups brought out this trait even more. From the moment Matsi met Wahots, Wyakin, and Chemukh, he was determined to protect them, to be their guardian.

When the pups were young, Matsi was especially protective of them at mealtime. If Motomo or Amani got too close to one of the precious youngsters, Matsi snarled until the adult backed off.

The beta wolf had another way to make sure the pups got enough to eat.

When most of the carcass had been consumed, Matsi often led the pups away to the willows. They instinctively started whining and licking Matsi's mouth. Suddenly his whole body started heaving. A moment later he regurgitated a huge pile of partially digested meat, which the pups gladly gobbled up.

As gross as it seems, Matsi's unselfish act assured that the pups received the food they needed to grow, even at the expense of finishing his own meal. It was a beautiful example of the strong family bonds within the pack.

Every wolf in the Sawtooth Pack had a role to play. While Matsi was the serious, protective puppy sitter, Amani was the goofy uncle. His personality was a bit clownish to begin with, and even more so when it came to the pups.

Amani loved nothing more than to let the pups climb all over him and tug at his fur. Then he would chase them around until they turned the tables on him and he became the one being chased. I don't know if Amani would have given up a meal for the young wolves, but when it came to playtime, he provided barrels of fun.

These relationships and personalities were exactly what we wanted to show in our new film. One of our objectives was to bring the audience face-to-face with a wolf. That meant more than looking a wolf in the eyes. It meant looking *behind* the eyes, in a sense, to discover what that wolf is really like. We were finally capturing on film what it means to be a wolf.

The Sawtooth Pack had revealed much to us, but much more was to come. Soon we would see a side of the family that was more intense, more loving, and more surprising than we had ever expected. 🐾

## CHAPTER 13
# CELEBRATION!

## JAMIE

As the project entered the winter of its sixth year, the Sawtooth Pack had grown to a family of eight lively adults. Days and nights were filled with adventure, discovery, and contentment.

Sadly, this magical life couldn't go on forever.

The Forest Service granted a one-year extension of our permit to use the land, which would be up at the end of the summer. There was absolutely no way to extend it.

Jim always knew the pack would need a permanent home when the film project was completed. The Nez Perce tribe of northern Idaho had offered the perfect place, but it would take time to arrange and build a suitable enclosure. Knowing that our time with the wolves would end soon, we set out to make our final year with them our very best.

Over the years, the wolves had shown us much about how they live—how they play, how they settle disputes, how they maintain order, how they care for one another. But there was one very important part of life in a wolf pack that had eluded us. And we were hoping that now, finally, we could witness perhaps the most exciting time in the hidden lives of wolves.

Early winter is the breeding season in a wolf's world. That fact didn't mean much to the Sawtooth Pack until January of the project's final year.

Both Wyakin and Chemukh, the pack's only females, were of age to breed. Kamots would be the breeding male, that much was certain. He would choose his mate, and that wolf would become the alpha female.

Jim and I had little doubt that the chosen one would be Wyakin. Female breeding rights usually have to be fought for. The female that dominates her competition typically wins favor with her potential mate. Wyakin had dominated Chemukh from the time they were puppies.

Kamots also didn't seem very fond of Chemukh.

A few weeks after the pups had joined the pack, Kamots made it clear that Chemukh would have to wait her turn at mealtimes. We were shocked. Pups are given special treatment, and that includes eating first, along with the alpha. Such was the case for Wyakin and Wahots, but not for Chemukh. She had to eat last, along with Lakota. Jim and I wondered if picking on the shy wolf was a way to toughen her up and make her more assertive, behavior needed for survival. Maybe such "tough love" has a place in wolf society.

I don't know if what we witnessed was the result of tough love or the rude awakening of a sleeping personality trait, but at the end of January, Chemukh's "inner wolf" roared onto the scene.

She turned from the most timid to the most aggressive. It was as if she realized she was running last in this race and needed to turn on the afterburners to blast ahead.

Chemukh started to join the pack as they tormented Lakota, something she had rarely done before. Now she seemed to be making up for lost time. She tore into the poor omega with a vengeance. Instead of dominating him with growls and pinning, like the others did, she grabbed his thigh and shook it violently until his yelps of pain called her off.

But she saved her most savage attacks for Wyakin. Chemukh quickly ran and launched herself at the gray female, clamping down on her rump time and time again. Wyakin was no match for Chemukh's new-found aggression.

The behavior of the other wolves was changing, too. Matsi, Motomo, and Amani were becoming especially antsy. They walked around with a nervous energy, sensing something important was about to happen.

Soon, Kamots would need to choose.

Jim and I secretly hoped he would choose Wyakin, who despite her history of dominating Chemukh was really a sweet, gentle wolf. We could easily see her as the mother of a new litter.

But if living with wolves taught us anything, it is that wolf behavior is complex beyond our understanding. Just when you think you have them figured out, they surprise you.

Kamots chose Chemukh.

Chemukh had once been in danger of becoming the omega female. Now she was the alpha female. What a turn of events!

Having won the heart of Kamots, Chemukh suddenly became sweet and loving. The pair spent nearly every minute of the day together. They walked together, sat together, and lay down together. I remember Jim filming Chemukh on her back with her legs curled up in the air while Kamots gently nuzzled her chin. They were snuggling. It was a heartwarming portrait of tenderness.

Such were the rituals of courtship. Would they lead to the first pups born to the Sawtooth Pack? It was too early to tell. Female wolves have seven days, a relatively small window of opportunity, to become pregnant.

Throughout that intense week, Kamots had to keep an eye on the other males, because they were keeping their eyes on Chemukh. If another male happened to wander too close to her, Kamots drove him away with a ferocity we had never seen from the proud alpha.

He didn't have to worry about Wahots and Lakota. The omega wanted no part of all this drama and kept his distance. Wahots was watchful and curious about the courtship, but he didn't express any desire to mate.

Matsi, Motomo, and Amani were a different story. They howled, paced, and howled some more, day and night. Tempers were short and the usual pack greetings were replaced with serious looks and snarls. You could cut the tension with a knife.

One day during a rare moment when Kamots was away from Chemukh's side, Motomo approached the alpha female. Wahots saw the scene unfold and let out a strange combination of a bark and a howl.

I was familiar with every sound Wahots ever made, but this was a new one for me. It was an SOS. Kamots heard it and came charging. In a rage he threw himself at Motomo, knocking him into a somersault and sending him running for the woods.

The young Wahots was tattling on Motomo, but why? I think he simply couldn't stand the idea of Motomo violating the rules of the pack. I imagined Wahots saying, "Not on *my* watch."

As the snow started melting in early April, we knew that Chemukh was pregnant. The telltale sign wasn't an extended belly; it was her behavior. She started digging.

One afternoon she dug a hole next to a boulder and another next to the base of a tree. The next day she dug a few more holes, all in different spots. We followed her as she inspected rock after rock, tree after tree.

We realized that she was searching for a site to dig a den—a place to give birth to her pups!

Finding and digging such a den is the job of the mother-to-be, and it had to be just right. Chemukh was very particular. She would dig beneath a log for a while and then abandon the site. Something must not have been to her liking. Maybe the soil was too wet or too rocky or something else was off about the area, and the search would continue.

The other wolves also started digging shallow pits all over the enclosure. They weren't helping. They were just caught up in the spirit of the event they knew was coming.

Chemukh finally found the perfect site.

It was in a wooded area on high ground at the far end of the territory. A fallen spruce had formed a hollow space between the ground and the trunk. It was a good location, but it must have been a fixer-upper, because Chemukh spent several days digging and scraping inside the hollow space. She would disappear into the blackness and within seconds clumps of dirt came flying out.

The other wolves were ready to burst with excitement. It was no longer life as usual; this was something special. You could feel the anticipation.

Then, one evening, Chemukh slipped away quietly from the rest of the pack ...

When we awoke the next morning, no wolves were in sight. I looked at Jim and said, "This is it!"

We threw on some clothes and rushed up to the spruce grove. The pack was gathered around the den, whining and shifting their weight from one front paw to the other. We were careful not to disturb the wolves, so we watched from afar. Then over the next hour we quietly approached the den.

From somewhere deep inside the darkness came the tiny squeals of newborn pups.

We were brimming with glee, but the wolves were having a full-blown celebration. When they weren't near the den site listening to the newborns' squeaks and squeals, they were whirling around in energetic play. When Chemukh emerged from the den later that morning, each wolf greeted her warmly.

We were glad to see that Chemukh was well, but what everyone really wanted to see—wolves and humans alike—were the newborn pups. That would have to wait a little while longer. The den was the domain of the mother and her young. No other wolf, not even Kamots, was allowed to enter.

So, I was incredibly honored when later that day I approached the den and Chemukh emerged, licked my nose, and sat down beside me. She seemed to be inviting me to visit her pups, and I accepted with great humility. The wolf that I had helped raise two years earlier trusted me with all that was most precious to her.

And that is why I crawled into a dark, mysterious hole in the ground with a large, powerful wolf sitting calmly beside me.

I took out a small flashlight and let Chemukh inspect it. Then I wormed my way headfirst into the den.

The hole was the entrance to a tunnel almost six feet (2 m) long and barely wide enough for me to fit comfortably inside. Small roots dangled from the ceiling like cobwebs.

As I wriggled through the den, I marveled at Chemukh's handiwork. The tunnel curved slightly left and opened up into a larger area. At the very back of the den, Chemukh had carved out a shelf to keep her pups off the damp ground. There, huddled against the far wall, was a wiggly mass of black fur.

It took me a moment to distinguish three individual heads. Their newborn eyes were still closed. They whined, chirped, and sniffed the air, no doubt wondering what this strange new scent was and if it meant that food was on its way.

I realized that I was looking into the faces of the first wolves born in the Sawtooth Mountains in 50 years. These little furry creatures in the beam of my flashlight were Sawtooth through and through.

The smell inside also surprised me. I was expecting a strong animal odor. But all my human nose could detect was the pleasant musty scent of fresh spring soil. Chemukh knew to keep a clean den so as not to attract bears, coyotes, or other predators.

My visit lasted less than a minute, but it was long enough to be the thrill of a lifetime. I backed out of the tunnel slowly and emerged covered in dirt. Chemukh again licked my nose. Then she disappeared back into the den.

I wonder if she understood how grateful I was.

Chemukh stayed in or around the den for a week or so, choosing to remain with her pups rather than join the pack to feast on the latest roadkill. But the pack made sure she wouldn't go hungry.

Kamots chewed off a deer leg and dragged it to the den. Wyakin brought her food as well.

Wyakin was especially attentive to the new mother. She spent most of her time sitting outside the den, just in case Chemukh or the pups needed her. It was hard to believe that Wyakin had been Chemukh's mortal enemy only two months before. But that observation is from a human's viewpoint. From a wolf's, they weren't enemies at all. Competitors, yes; enemies, never.

As the chill of April gave way to the warmth of May, Chemukh decided it was time to introduce her pups to the great outdoors, and to the pack.

She carried them out of the den one by one and set them on a sunny patch of grass. Their blue eyes had just opened; each had black fur, like their mother. The pups had not gotten used to standing on their wobbly legs, but they crawled around and sniffed at everything they could reach.

The adults moved from one pup to another whining, sniffing, and inspecting. Then they walked over to Chemukh to pay their respects. It was yet another scene of affection and tenderness that few people would ever have attributed to wolves.

I could see how happy Jim was. It had been his dream from the beginning of the project to have a litter born within the pack and to witness the response of the other wolves. That dream was being fulfilled.

Throughout the spring, each wolf responded to the pups in different ways. Chemukh quickly grew tired of parenting and left such duties to Wyakin, who was all too happy to step in. She watched over the pups and cleaned them with her tongue. When Chemukh returned to nurse, Wyakin stepped back, but she was always available as the loving aunt.

Kamots established order and discipline. Matsi became the puppies' caretaker and puppy sitter, as he had been for Chemukh herself, as well as Wahots and Wyakin.

And of course, Amani continued to be the favorite uncle. He was even more playful with the Sawtooth litter than he had been previously. He would lie down and let the pups attack him. One would yank his tail, another would pull on his ears, and a third would nip at his neck. To the pups, Amani was a giant chew toy, and he didn't mind a bit.

As we had done with the other litters, we spent time socializing the pups to people. This was essential. Even after the project was complete, the pack would be moving to a new enclosure to live out their lives on tribal lands of the Nez Perce. So, we needed to spend several critical weeks providing them with the same kind of care the earlier pups had received.

As always, we enjoyed the task of naming the pack's newest additions. We gave two of them Nez Perce names. The male was Piyip (PIE-yip), or "boy." One of the females was Ayet (eye-YET), or "girl."

Jim named the other female Motaki, after the wolf that had been killed by a cougar four years earlier. It was a fitting tribute to one of the sweetest, most playful wolves of the pack, and a symbol that the pack had come full circle.

Watching and filming the Sawtooth litter that spring and summer was bittersweet. Piyip, Ayet, and Motaki brought out behaviors and emotions in the pack that we hadn't experienced before. Yet we knew our days to enjoy such experiences were numbered.

Soon, we would have to part with our dear friends. 🐾

## CHAPTER 14

# TIME TO SAY GOODBYE

## JAMIE

July was the last full month that we would have with the Sawtooth Pack, and we decided to make the most of it. We left our filming equipment behind and just spent every minute we could with the wolves. We wanted to memorize their every move, expression, and sound so that our experiences with them would be forever in our minds.

Every day, I spent some time with Lakota. I told him how sad I was to leave him but that I would visit often. I told him that two of his friends from wolf camp—part of our crew—would be with him at his new home.

"Everything will be all right," I said over and over, though deep in my heart I knew that wasn't completely true. How could it be when I was certain I would miss him so very, very much.

He reached up and placed his paw on my shoulder. I reached across my body and placed my hand on his paw. Friends forever.

One of the most special moments of those final days also became one of the most magical, unforgettable moments of my life.

I was sitting near a group of willows where I often met with Lakota. But instead of a visit from the omega, the alpha came over and sat down beside me. Our bodies were almost touching.

Suddenly Kamots began to howl. The awesome power of his voice filled the air around us. It seemed to fill the world. There was nothing else but this wolf and his song.

Without thinking, I did something I had never done before or since. I reached up and gently placed my hand on his throat.

The sensation was electric. Vibrations shot up my arm, filled my entire body, and shook the ground beneath me. I felt like a thrumming conduit between the wolf and the earth. So I closed my eyes and let the wolf song flow through me.

In that moment, I understood more than ever what it means to be a wolf. I *felt* the unity of the pack, the connection with the land, and the freedom of the wild.

I will always be grateful to Kamots for giving me this very special gift.

## JIM

That late summer day dawned bright and sunny, but our hearts were heavy. It was the last day in wolf camp for the Sawtooth Pack. The aluminum crates in which the wolves would be transported sat in the enclosure, placed there so that the pack would become accustomed to them. Those silvery boxes seemed so out of place, so ugly, so wrong. Yet, we knew what had to be done.

In the late afternoon, the wolves were each given a piece of meat that contained a light sedative to prepare them for a tranquilizer to knock them out completely. That was the only way to get the wolves into the crates. Then, we would start the trip once they woke.

Kamots resisted the effects of the drug longer than the others and needed a second dose, but eventually he fell asleep. As alpha, he had more fight in him than the others, knowing the safety of the pack rested with him. We placed each adult wolf in a separate crate, while the three four-month-old Sawtooth pups shared one.

One of the crew members moved from crate to crate, monitoring the sleeping wolves' breathing and heart rate until the sedative wore off. All vital signs were normal except for that of Kamots. His heartbeat was faint and irregular. His breathing was shallow. Though we had given him more than the rest of the pack, he had had only a fraction of the dosage that government veterinarians routinely administer to wild wolves when they sedate them. Yet, Kamots was reacting badly to the drug.

Was something wrong? We were worried, but all we could do was wait.

An hour went by and the sedative started to wear off. The wolves woke up one by one. They shook off their grogginess and sat up in their crates.

All but Kamots.

Finally, after many anxious minutes, his ears twitched and his eyes opened. But he was still dazed and didn't get up.

We thought it best to start the journey even though Kamots was not fully awake. The enclosure on the Nez Perce lands was in northern Idaho, not terribly far as the crow flies, but a 10-hour drive on winding roads. We decided we would stop several times along the way to keep a close eye on Kamots.

So, we carefully loaded the crates into a horse trailer, and in the golden glow of sunset we pulled out across the ranchlands.

Thus began the saddest trip we have ever taken. We were leaving the life that Jamie and I, and the wolves, had created together over many years.

Less than an hour into the trip, we stopped to check on the wolves. They were all alert and sitting in their crates—again, except for Kamots. He still lay motionless.

I reached in through the bars on the gate and stroked his neck. I spoke gently.

"I'm so sorry, Kamots. It's going to be okay. I promise." Jamie whispered between sniffles, "Kamots, please wake up. Your family needs you. We can't do this without you."

We drove for another hour before pulling over again. I opened the door of the trailer slowly, afraid of what I might find.

There was Kamots sitting up in the crate! We had never been so relieved. I placed my hand by the gate and Kamots licked my fingers. He was going to be fine, and I felt the pack would be, too.

We drove all night, stopping often to check on the wolves and to assure them that they would soon be at their new home and everything was going to be all right.

After a long journey, we finally pulled up to the new enclosure. At sunrise we walked the perimeter to make sure the fencing was secure. Then we carried the crates into the enclosure and lined them up in a field of knee-high grass.

We let the pups out first so that the adults would see that they were safe. Piyip, Ayet, and Motaki leaped out into the grass. They explored only a short distance from the crates before looking back and waiting for their family.

Next out was Kamots. He seemed a bit uncertain for a moment, but then went over to the pups, who greeted him enthusiastically. Ayet ran over to Matsi in his crate and licked his nose through the bars. Matsi was released next and greeted Ayet while Piyip and Motaki ran to him.

We released the other adults in quick succession, with each greeting the pups and then Kamots.

Only Lakota remained in his crate. We let him out last to follow the social order that the wolves themselves had long ago established. The gate was open, but he remained inside, unsure if it was safe to come out.

The rest of the pack was about to begin exploring their new home when Kamots realized that the family was missing a member. He looked back and saw Lakota cowering in the crate. Kamots returned to his brother and the two whined back and forth.

After a while, Lakota poked his nose out and sniffed the air. Then he slowly set one paw onto the grass, and then another, before rushing to the alpha. Kamots pressed his shoulder against Lakota's and the two walked side by side into the meadow. It was one of the most touching gestures I've ever seen. Lakota needed encouragement and reassurance, and his loving brother and devoted leader provided it.

Jamie and I sat in the grass and watched the wolves trot off to explore every corner of the enclosure. I was glad to see that while the location had changed, the unity of their family remained intact. Apparently, home was wherever the wolves were, as long as they were together.

We stayed with the wolves for two days to make sure they were adjusting to their new home. Then it was time to say goodbye.

The morning of our departure, Jamie and I sat in the meadow as the wolves gathered around us. One by one we said farewell. We told them how much we would miss them and that we would always think of them. We told them we loved them.

It was difficult to say goodbye to any of the wolves, but especially Lakota, Kamots, and Matsi. They had come to symbolize what we treasure most about wolves—the love and devotion that keeps a pack together. They taught us that wolf nature is not that different from our own.

As they trotted off to begin their day, I knew the pack didn't realize we were leaving. To them, our "goodbye" was a "good morning." It was the same kind of greeting they always gave us when they first saw us each day. They fully expected to see us tomorrow.

But we would be gone, and it tore at my heart that they would not understand why.

Jamie and I held hands as the pack disappeared around a bend. Then we embraced and let the tears flow. We were sad, to be sure, but also grateful and joyful.

The Sawtooth Pack had shown us so much. They had placed their story in our hands and entrusted us to spread the word, to speak their truth to an audience they could not reach themselves. That was the ultimate trust the wolves placed in us. We cherished it then as we cherish it now.

The summer and fall passed, and after four months, we made the first of many visits to the pack. We were excited to see them but also a bit nervous. Would they remember us, or would they think of us as strangers?

Kamots provided the answer.

He first saw us from across a snow-covered meadow. There was a moment of hesitation, as if he couldn't quite believe who it was.

Then he came rushing through the snow, followed by the rest of the pack.

They nearly knocked us off our feet as they leaped up and smothered us with those very special wolf kisses. It was like the fluffy tornado that Jamie had experienced when she first arrived at wolf camp.

We were so gratified that after all this time, the wolves still welcomed us. The trust we had built up over the years was alive and well.

So was their affection. From the exuberance of their greeting, it was clear that they had missed us. It was also clear that they weren't angry with us for leaving them.

But then again, why would they be angry? They had one another. Wolves don't hold grudges. Wolves forgive.

Over the years, we visited as often as we could. And when we couldn't, our two caretakers who had moved with the wolves kept us up to date on how the pack was doing. On that special first visit, we were overjoyed to learn that Lakota was no longer the omega. Wahots had taken over that position, allowing Lakota to retire. We could only imagine how relieved Lakota was. We heard that he never picked on the new omega. Somehow, we knew he wouldn't.

Wolves typically live only seven to 10 years, and over time, members of the Sawtooth Pack left us. I was devastated when I found out that Kamots had died. For three weeks afterward a single wolf was heard howling in the night. In all likelihood, it was his devoted brother, Lakota.

The last wolf to pass was Piyip. He died in 2013 at the incredibly old age of 17. We posted his passing on social media, and evidently the Sawtooth Pack has a lot of friends. In one day, 98,000 people shared his story.

As flesh-and-blood animals, the members of the Sawtooth Pack now exist only in our memories. But in a very real way, they live on.

Because they accepted us into their lives, these animals allowed us to show the human world a side of wolves that few people knew existed. Wolves are more than efficient hunters. They are more than animals of superb beauty and strength. They are intelligent. They care for one another. They value friendship and trust. Above all, they have compassion.

A wolf pack is a family. It's a caring and confident leader, a playful and peacemaking omega. It's devoted aunts and uncles that watch over young ones. It's brothers and sisters getting into all sorts of trouble. It's individuals with a yearning to belong to something bigger than themselves.

Every time a person thinks about wolves with this new understanding, Kamots, Lakota, Matsi, and the rest of the Sawtooth Pack live on. They will always be with us. 🐾

# EPILOGUE

## JIM AND JAMIE

One autumn day, a few years after the project ended, we took a trip back to the site of wolf camp. It was an emotional journey.

We had long since removed every structure; no traces of camp or the fence remained. Natural landmarks, however, were everywhere, and they brought back vivid memories.

We passed the spruce grove where Jim had brought smuggled food to Makuyi and became her only friend. We strolled through the meadow where the wolves had always played. We visited the den that Jamie had disappeared into and where Jim had stood in disbelief. Memories came flooding back—of our tiny yurt, the woodstove, and our friends, the Sawtooth Pack.

As we continued our wanderings along the creek that led to the ponds, our boots squished in patches of mud and snow.

That's when we looked down and saw them.

Wolf tracks.

For a brief moment, these marks in the snow didn't register as anything unusual. We had been used to seeing wolf tracks all over the place in this area. But then the obvious dawned on us: These tracks were *not* from the Sawtooth Pack.

We examined the large, fresh paw prints. Our eyes danced. Broad smiles lit up our faces. A wild wolf had passed through here in recent days, probably a large male from the size of the tracks. Wild wolves were back in the Sawtooth Mountains for the first time in nearly 60 years!

He was most likely from a pack farther north and was traveling south to find a mate and start a new pack. We wondered what he thought when he picked up the fading scent of the Sawtooth Pack. We hoped that he felt comfortable here. We hoped that he recognized this area as wolf country.

Above all, we hoped that here, among the lingering traces of the wolves who shared their lives with us, he felt like he belonged. 🐾

# THE WORLD OF THE WOLF

Today, gray wolves are one of two species that live in North America; the other is the red wolf, of which there are only an estimated 40 left in the wild. Four other gray wolf subspecies include the Mexican wolf, the arctic wolf, the Plains wolf, and the northern timber wolf. And recently, a new species of wolf was discovered in Africa, the African golden wolf.

Greenland
(Denmark)

Alaska
(U.S.)

Pacific
Ocean

CANADA

**MAP KEY**

Where gray
wolves lived in
North America
before 1800

UNITED STATES

Atlantic
Ocean

🐾 **HISTORICALLY, GRAY WOLVES LIVED IN MOST AREAS OF NORTH AMERICA,** throughout Canada, Alaska, most of the continental United States, and as far south as southern Mexico. However, in the late 1800s, American settlers pushed west, straight into wolf territory. Eventually, the government employed hunters to kill thousands of wolves every year. By the 1970s, gray wolf populations were at an all-time low and in 1973 Congress passed the Endangered Species Act, protecting the gray wolf.

MEXICO

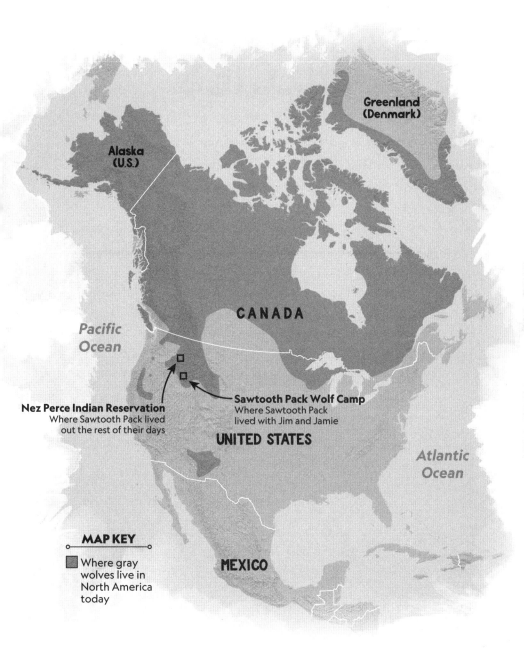

Greenland
(Denmark)

Alaska
(U.S.)

Pacific
Ocean

CANADA

**Nez Perce Indian Reservation**
Where Sawtooth Pack lived
out the rest of their days

**Sawtooth Pack Wolf Camp**
Where Sawtooth Pack
lived with Jim and Jamie

UNITED STATES

Atlantic
Ocean

**MAP KEY**

■ Where gray
wolves live in
North America
today

MEXICO

🐾 **UNDER THE PROTECTIONS OF THE ENDANGERED SPECIES ACT,** wolves began to
recover in the American West and Great Lakes region. And even though it's only been a short
time since wolves have called the West home again, scientists are seeing positive changes to
ecosystems. However, recent laws have removed wolves from endangered species protection in
several states. In those places, these fragile populations are again in decline.

# KEYSTONE SPECIES

Gray wolves were hunted nearly to extinction in the American West during the 19th and 20th centuries. But, they've been reintroduced to central Idaho and Yellowstone National Park and are now making a comeback.

Our understanding of wolves and their role in their ecosystem has changed significantly in the past three decades. Wolves are considered a keystone species, meaning that their habitat is dependent on them to keep the balance. And when wolves were reintroduced to Yellowstone, scientists began to notice some incredible changes.

## 🐾 WITHOUT WOLVES

When there were no wolves in Yellowstone National Park between 1926 and 1995, the ecosystem drastically changed. With few predators around, elk lost their fear of being hunted. As a result, overbrowsing by elk meant that tree saplings never had the chance to grow into mature trees. The elk also gathered near streams and ate the shrubs by the banks that helped prevent erosion. Birds lost nesting space. And habitats for fish, amphibians, and reptiles were damaged as streams became broader, shallower, and warmer.

### 🐾 WITH WOLVES

Now that wolves are back in Yellowstone, elk numbers in the park have decreased and their behavior has changed. They are spending less time lingering near streams, and more time on higher ground, where they are safer from predators, allowing trees and streamside shrubs relief to grow strong. And now that wolves are back in their natural habitat, their leftovers from kills provide food for scavengers, such as bald and golden eagles, badgers, and bears.

# ABOUT
# LIVING WITH
# WOLVES

During the wolf project, we produced three documentaries about the Sawtooth Pack, which were successful beyond our wildest dreams. After sharing the pack's story, we watched as these amazing animals became wolf ambassadors, showing people the true, but previously unseen, nature of wolves.

But we knew we had to do something more. Living with the pack left a permanent mark on us. The Sawtooth Pack gave us so much and their wild cousins were still so misunderstood. We knew we needed to be a voice for wolves everywhere. By creating our nonprofit organization, Living with Wolves, we found a new way to speak up for them and to give others inspired by the Sawtooth Pack a way to join us on this journey.

Living with Wolves is dedicated to the study of wolves and wolf habitats and to seeking solutions for coexistence. Our aim is to educate the public worldwide and promote the truth about wolves while inspiring people to help protect them. We support grassroots initiatives and campaigns to encourage wolf-protecting legislation and meet personally with state and federal government officials. We collaborate with researchers to study human impacts on wolves, and we create exhibits, presentations, magazine articles, and books to reach as many people as possible.

All of this is just the beginning of our mission. The return of wolves to the American West is a great success story. But ever since wolves were removed from the endangered species list in some places, they are being hunted and trapped at an alarming rate. The war against the wolf continues.

Join us in our fight to protect these amazing animals. You'll find yourself among the many thousands of other concerned people who understand the importance of taking a stand—for wolves, and for a world where they can continue to play their important role and live without persecution.

## HOW YOU CAN HELP

### 🐾 STUDY UP

With the help of a parent, visit our website: *livingwithwolves.org*. It's full of wonderful photos, reliable information, and an amazing interactive exhibit. Plus, we'll keep you up to date on how you can help protect wolves and provide good ideas about how to help. You'll also find the latest information, research, and field reports about wolves and conservation efforts around the globe. For real-time updates, ask a parent for permission to check us out on social media.

### 🐾 SPEAK OUT

Be a voice for wolves by letting lawmakers and wildlife managers know that you care about the decisions they make. Meetings are held regularly in wildlife offices at all levels of national and state government. Check out our website for information on who represents you, and the best way to contact them when wolf issues are being discussed. They need to hear smart, rational input from all of us!

### 🐾 RAISE AWARENESS

With a parent's help, consider hosting a local fund-raiser or an event—such as a bake sale—to benefit wolves. Include brochures or handouts with information on wolves, and then donate the funds to a nonprofit organization that supports them.

### 🐾 MAKE A CHANGE

Use your knowledge about wolves to start a petition. Start by researching a law or change that could help wolves. Identify a senior decision-maker, such as a politician, who can help to make the change needed, and address your petition to them. A parent can help you collect signatures for your petition, or even put it online. Then send the petition!

**Together, we know we can make effective and lasting change for wolves a reality.**

# ACKNOWLEDGMENTS

We are so grateful to the following people for providing support, ideas, and advice on the care of wolves, on the making of three documentaries, and on the writing of this book: Ed Bangs, Peter Bricca, Dave Dickie, Norma Douglas, Joe Fontaine, Steve Fritts, Nelson Funk, Jack Furey, Gary Gadwa, Jim and Lucia Gilliland, Jed Gray, Gordon Haber, Jeremy Heft, Kate Hopkins, Maurice Hornocker, Mike Jimenez, David Knotts, the Nez Perce tribe, David O'Dell, Carl Pence, Evelyn B. Phillips, Lou Racine, Mose Richards, and Eric Zimmen.

Thank you also to the team at National Geographic Kids: our editor, Kate Hale, who encouraged us to tell this story for a young audience; art director Sanjida Rashid; photo editor Shannon Hibberd; and the production, marketing, and publicity teams.

This project would have been much more difficult without the support of our dear friends and family. Too numerous to mention here, you all know who you are, thank you.

A very special thanks to the crews of *Wolf: Return of a Legend*, *Wolves at Our Door*, and *Living With Wolves*. These individuals lived and worked with us at wolf camp as part of the filmmaking team or as caretakers for the Sawtooth Pack (the lines between the two jobs were often blurred): Sarah Bingaman, Christina Dutcher, Garrick Dutcher, Johann Guschelbauer, Janet Kellam, Keith Marshall, Megan Parker, Bob Poole, Jake Provonsha, Patty Provonsha, Burke Smith, and Shane Stent.

Lastly, this book, the wolf project, and the films would never have happened without the support and vision of four very important people, to whom we owe a special debt of gratitude: Dennis Kane, James Manfull, Glen Phelan, and Karin Rundquist.